A Portrait of Everyday Life in Wisconsin

This book was made possible in part through generous support from:

Wisconsin
You're Among Friends

Sponsored By A Special Grant From
The Professional Photography Division Of
EASTMAN KODAK COMPANY

Patterson Communications, Inc.

These companies have also generously
supported this book:

MCP COMPANY, INC.

N & M TRANSFER CO., INC.

NORTHWESTERN

Northwestern Colorgraphics Inc.
A Banta Corporation Subsidiary

phopar

A Schneider National Company

Insurance and Related Financial Services

Worzalla Publishing
Company

Previous page

Adams County
Keith Myers

This page and next

Brown County
Curt Knoke

Credits

Produced and Directed by:
Elsie E. Patterson
Susan J. Hoffmann
Chief Photo Editor:
Leroy "Skip" Zacher
Art Director:
Beth Wenger-Marsh, Wenger-Marsh, Inc.
Designer:
Frank W. Meier, Wenger-Marsh, Inc.
Photo Editors:
Elsie E. Patterson
Susan J. Hoffmann
Beth Wenger-Marsh
Frank W. Meier
Biographies Editor:
Bonnie Auxier
Typesetting:
Frank W. Meier and
Mary Verboomen, Wenger-Marsh, Inc.
Photo Processor:
Phopar, Appleton
Electronic Imaging
Pisani/Wilson Studio, Green Bay and Appleton
Color Separators:
Pages 1 - 64:
MCP Company, Inc., Milwaukee
Pages 65 - 128:
OEC Graphics, Oshkosh
Pages 129 - 192:
Digital Color, Menomonee Falls
Pages 193 - 256
Northwestern Colorgraphics, Inc., Menasha
Jacket:
Northwestern Colorgraphics, Inc., Menasha
Printer/Binder:
Worzalla Publishing Company, Stevens Point
Individual Book Cartons:
Great Northern Corporation, Appleton
Body Stock:
80 lb. white Consolith Gloss Enamel
Jacket:
CIS Litho, UV coating.
Henshel Coating, New Berlin
Distributed by:
Perin Press, Appleton

Published by Patterson Communications, Inc., Neenah, WI

Library of Congress Cataloging-in-publication Data main
entry under title:
A Portrait of Everyday Life in Wisconsin
Captions, narrative, biographies by: Elsie E. Patterson

ISBN 0-9620583-0-0 $35.95

1. Wisconsin - Social life and customs - Pictorial works.
2. Wisconsin - Description and travel - 1981 - Views.
I. Patterson, Elsie E., 1935-
F582.P67 1988
977.5 '043' 0222--dc19   88-20002   CIP

Project Directors: Elsie E. Patterson and Susan J. Hoffmann
Printed in Wisconsin   First Printing August 1988

10 9 8 7 6 5 4 3 2 1

Major Sponsors:
Wisconsin Division of Tourism Development
Eastman Kodak, Rochester, NY

Major Contributors:
Clifton, Gunderson & Co., Neenah
Digital Color, Menomonee Falls
MCP Company, Inc., Milwaukee
N & M Transfer Company, Inc. Neenah
Northwestern Colorgraphics, Menasha
OEC Graphics, Oshkosh
Phopar, Appleton
Schneider Communications, Green Bay
Secura Insurance, Appleton
Worzalla Publishing Company, Stevens Point

Contributors:
ABC Supply Co. Inc., Beloit
Allen-Bradley, Milwaukee
Associated Banc-Corp., Green Bay
Milt and Joanne Benner, Oshkosh
Cablevision of the Fox Cities, Appleton
Camera Casino, Oshkosh
Carver Boat Corporation, Pulaski
*Conkey's Bookstore, Appleton
Contract Services, Menomonee Falls
The Copps Corporation, Stevens Point
Employers Health Insurance, De Pere
Bob and Gini Ernest, Neenah
George Webb Restaurants-Wisconsin's largest locally
    owned restaurant chain
Great Northern Corporation, Appleton
GTE North Incorporated, Sun Prairie
Gundersen Clinic, Ltd., La Crosse
Henschel Coating, New Berlin
Leon Hoffmann, Insurance Specialist, Oshkosh
The Ink Spot, Appleton
David Johnson, Oshkosh
Michael Johnson, Oshkosh
Tim Johnson, Oshkosh
Sally and Jim Keating, Neenah
Herbert Kohl, Milwaukee
Kohler Co., Kohler
*Koss Corporation, Milwaukee
Krause Publications, Iola
Lands' End, Inc., Dodgeville
Marathon Cheese Corporation, Marathon
Marathon Engineers/Architects/Planners, Menasha
Marshall Field's, Wisconsin
Maxair Incorporated, Appleton
McGraw Painting and Decorating, Oshkosh
Mercury Marine, Fond du Lac
Midwest Express Airlines, Inc., Milwaukee
*Mid-Western Sport Togs, Berlin
Morgan and Myers, Jefferson
*Narada, Milwaukee
Norwest Bank Minnesota N.A.-Wisconsin Division
Office Technology, Inc., Neenah
Overall Communications, Inc., Oshkosh
Peterson Builders, Inc., Sturgeon Bay
*Presto Products, Inc., Appleton
Beverly Rindfleisch, Neenah
*Sportsman of Berlin, Ltd., Berlin
*Valley School and Office Suppliers, Inc., Appleton
The West Bend Company, West Bend
Wisconsin Bell, Madison
Wisconsin Dairies, Baraboo
Wisconsin Physicians Service, Madison
Wisconsin Southern Gas Company, Lake Geneva
Wisconsin Tissue Mills Inc., Menasha

*provided honorariums for photographers

Friends and Advisors:
David Aronson
Bonnie Auxier
Ric Ballin
Paul Baudhuin
Dale Bachim
John S. Biro
Robert W. Brown
Sen. Carol Buettner
Dick Calder
Marigen Carpenter
Thom Ciske
Kathy Courtois
E. James Dreyer
Boris Frank Associates
Ruth Friese
Joel Garlock
Elizabeth Glass
Ruth Goetz
Glen and Sue Gunderson
Ron F. Hoerth
Britton Hoffmann
Leon Hoffmann
Matthew Hoffmann
Nicole Hoffmann
William "Butch" Johnson
Sen. Robert Kasten
Sally Keating
Tom Klein
Ginny Kline
Jim Koepnick
Mark Koth
Dick Matty
Oshkosh Public Library Information Desk
Benjamin Patterson
Gene Patterson
Jeffrey P. Patterson
Melinda Patterson
Tom Pawlacyk
Kay Pharmakis
Larry Pynch
Oswald Rapp
Dick Reinhart
Beverly Rindfleisch
Dick Rutledge
Jack Schloesser
Bob Schulze
Carl Schuppel
David Schwartz
Paul Stevenson
Gov. Tommy G. Thompson
Boyd Tracy
Helen Urch
Ronald L. Van De Hey
David Varney
Virginia Walker
Philip Weston
Katherine Westover
Larry Wirth
Marlene Zacher
John Zimmerman

Dane County
Gary Knowles

Project Directors' Notes

On Friday, May 6, 1988, a unique and historic event took place in Wisconsin: Seventy-five enthusiastic photographers devoted a day to capturing the essence of the state by photographing people in everyday life situations. Their instructions were to focus on the human element and photograph the ordinary and the outrageous; the traditional and the non-traditional; the young and the old; and the sad and the happy -- and they were to have fun doing it! A selection of the resulting photos would be the content of the book you are now holding.

Elsie and her husband Gene put twin-check numbers on rolls of film. All told, it took four people eight hours to number 1600 rolls of film.

Pre-news conference luncheon meeting at Inn on the Park, Madison. Left to right: Dick Matty, Elsie, Susan, John Zimmerman and Gary Knowles. John Zimmerman, Perin Press, Appleton, will distribute "Portrait".

It was Susan who, in January 1987, first suggested doing this book. The idea stemmed from the recent publication of a highly-successful series of photographic books using a similar format. Susan was convinced that Wisconsin, with its diverse people and lifestyles, was an ideal subject for a pictorial book. Up until this time, a number of books had focused on the scenery of Wisconsin, but none had featured the people.

Elsie Patterson and Dick Matty, administrator of tourism development, at the May 2 news conference in the Governor's Conference Room in the Capitol. The news conference was called to announce to the people of the state that on May 6, an historic state-wide event was going to take place.

We both knew that coordinating a project of this magnitude, and ultimately publishing the book, would be no small undertaking; but we also knew that it fell within the realm of our capabilities, and what we didn't already know, we could soon learn. Elsie, who has a degree in journalism, had left a corporate public relations job and opened Patterson Communications in the fall of 1986 to work as an independent advertising and public relations practitioner and freelance writer. Susan's three children were at an age where she felt she was ready to expand her horizons and get involved in some business activity outside the home. So, it appeared the timing was right for the two of us -- a mother and daughter team -- to undertake this project. The prospect of working together on a major project would be challenging and exciting.

Production photos by Skip Zacher unless otherwise noted.

In pursuing the book's possibilities, we talked with a number of professionals related to various aspects of the project, and we were encouraged by their enthusiastic responses. In the early stages of planning, we decided that not only would *A Portrait of Everyday Life in Wisconsin* feature Wisconsin's people, but the book would be produced entirely within the state. Wisconsin is one of the few states which has all the necessary capabilities required for book publishing, including production of the world's finest paper, photo processing, color separating, printing, binding and distribution. In its finished form, *A Portrait of Everyday Life in Wisconsin* would be an ideal means to exhibit the talents of Wisconsin's photographers, craftsmen and manufacturers.

We felt strongly that a book of this nature would have significant merit for the state of Wisconsin, and that belief was reinforced when the project received Governor Tommy G. Thompson's letter of endorsement and his official commendation which asked the people of the state to participate in the endeavor.

Governor Thompson's endorsement was supported by a recommendation from Dick Matty, administrator of tourism development. In addition, the Wisconsin Department of Development, Division of Tourism Development became a major sponsor of the project through its Joint Venture Program. It was merely a happy coincidence when the Division of Tourism unveiled its new tourism slogan "Wisconsin: You're Among Friends", which, in similarity to the emphasis of the book, focused on people rather than places.

Despite encouragement from everyone who learned of the project, there were a number of times we felt that the complexity and magnitude of the project, and the potential financial risk involved, would prohibit

On May 6, all participating photographers wore a white sweatshirt with a blue project logo. Model: Skip Zacher. Photographer: Elsie Patterson.

us from continuing. We knew the project was intrinsically good and, if at all possible, it should not be dropped. Each time feelings of discouragement arose, some form of support was forthcoming which spurred us on.

Maxair pilot Mike Paiser, Appleton, was kept busy flying Skip Zacher around Brown, Waupaca, Outagamie and Winnebago Counties.

In analyzing the prospect of publishing a book of this size and quality, it was clear that for it to be affordable to the general public, it would require financial backing. Weeks of planning and fundraising resulted in a number of Wisconsin businesses, and some individuals, becoming involved as sponsors and contributors. Eastman Kodak, Rochester, New York, became a major sponsor by donating 1600 rolls of Ektachrome film through a special grant from the Professional Photography Division.

Enthusiasm for the project became contagious following a statewide news release which we issued in January 1988. The media eagerly picked up on the announcement of the pending publication, and we were interviewed by our local television stations and did several radio/phone interviews throughout the state. The news release was also widely used in state newspapers and a business magazine and it generated a great deal of interest from photographers, potential corporate sponsors and residents of the state who felt it was time Wisconsin had a book like this.

Ozzie Rapp and Larry Pynch, co-owners of Phopar, review some of the 24,000 slides processed by their staff.

In the early stages of planning, Dr. Leroy "Skip" Zacher, professor of photojournalism at the University of Wisconsin -- Oshkosh, had agreed to serve as chief photo editor for the book. His first responsibility was to review resumes and portfolios which photographers submitted after learning of the unique photographic opportunity.

Beginning in September 1987, the project became a full-time occupation to the exclusion of any other business activities. As the project picked up momentum, it was necessary to juggle a variety of responsibilities. There were not enough hours in the day and it became commonplace to work nights and weekends. As spring approached, it was essential to continue fundraising, but the compressed time schedule -- we were aiming for an October publication date -- required that we firm up our production arrangements. It was also time to begin making the photographers' county assignments.

About 10 days before the scheduled shoot date, kits were shipped to the photographers. Each photographer was given 20 rolls of film which included 160, 400, P800/1600 ASAs and the new Kodak 100 Ektachrome Professional Plus.

Photographers were given general guidelines, and in only a few cases were there specific assignments. Once they were notified of their county assignments, they were free to make their own arrangements with the people they wanted to photograph.

In order to give the project a big send-off and let the people of the state know that something special was going to happen, we asked Dick Matty if he would call a news conference on behalf of the project. Dick graciously agreed, and on May 2, state media representatives were invited to the Governor's Conference Room in the Wisconsin Capitol to kick-off the event.

Beth Wenger-Marsh and Frank Meier discuss design and format with Elsie and Susan. Now begins the task of narrowing down the selection to approximately 300 photos.

On Friday, May 6, a brilliant moon gave way to a magnificent sunrise. As the people of Wisconsin woke on that glorious day and went about their normal activities, they welcomed the photographers into their homes, schools and work places, and invited them along during their leisure-time activities. *A Portrait of Everyday Life in Wisconsin* was, without a doubt, the most ambitious photojournalism assignment Wisconsin had ever experienced. In each of the state's 72 counties, typical everyday events were recorded through the eye of the camera and were made memorable in more than 24,000 photographs.

The photographers themselves were also the recipients of a good deal of attention, because newspaper, radio and television reporters and cameramen followed many of them around during some portion of the 24-hour assignment and shared their activities with the public. All in all, it was a wonderful, memorable day for everyone concerned.

For Britton, Matthew and Nicole, life changed when their mom, Susan, started working on the project. Meals were late, the laundry was never done on time, and car-pooling arrangements were often changed at the last minute. Nevertheless, they adjusted well and they were always excited about the book. Photographer: Elsie Patterson

At the heart of this book is a love of Wisconsin, an interest in people, and a curiosity about each other. Through more than 300 photographs contained on these pages, you are introduced to a representative sampling of the wonderful, interesting people who call Wisconsin their home.

Elsie E. Patterson
Susan J. Hoffmann

Photographers' County Assignments

* Leroy "Skip" Zacher had no specific assignment but was a "floater" and potential substitute.
** Richard Yehl substituted for Ilse Dietsche in Iron County. Ilse took selected photos in Wood and Waushara Counties.

Photographers' Biographies

Donald G. Albrecht
Bayfield, Wisconsin
As director of public relations at Northland College since 1983, Don has overseen and personally prepared many campus publications. He has also taught two photography courses "teaching others the technical skills and how to develop aesthetic taste in photography." Don's photos have been on display in many places including a one-man show at Northland College in 1983 entitled "Wrapped/Unwrapped." Several of his latest endeavors have been to produce a gourmet products brochure for the Old Rittenhouse Inn in Bayfield, Wisconsin, and to photograph five area musicians for an album cover.

Greg Anderson
Madison, Wisconsin
Raised in Thorp, Wisconsin, Greg went on to earn a degree at the University of Wisconsin-La Crosse in mass communications along with a photography minor. His work has been

Jackson County   **Mary "Casey" Martin**

published in the *Milwaukee Journal*, the *Milwaukee Sentinel* and *Newsweek* magazine. His photos have been on display at UW-La Crosse, Normandale Community College and the Science Museum of Minnesota. Currently, he is employed as a photographer for the University of Wisconsin-Madison in the photographic media center. Greg is called upon to photograph all aspects of college life. He describes his career as "short but very fun."

Bonnie Auxier
Neenah, Wisconsin
A 1987 graduate of the University of Wisconsin-Oshkosh with a major in photojournalism. Winner of over 35 awards in photography for excellence including the "Best of Show" award in the 1983 *Appleton Post-Crescent* Kodak International Newspaper Snapshot contest. Published three years in *The Best of Photography College Annual* printed and edited by Photographer's Forum in Santa Barbara, California. Bonnie's photos and articles have also been on the front pages of local newspapers. Her pictures have been on display at UW-Oshkosh, Menasha Public Library, Park Plaza in Oshkosh, the lobby of the *Post-Crescent* and the Hang-Up & Frame-Up Gallery in Neenah. She is currently a free-lance photographer and writer for area magazines. Bonnie works from her home in Neenah and is involved in a photo research project that could lead to a book.

Richard A. Ballin
Appleton, Wisconsin
A free-lance professional photographer who traveled to the Soviet Union in June 1987 to photograph the lives of people. His photos were compiled into an audio/visual program titled "WE WANT PEACE." These photos are currently being edited for a book by the same title. Ric, a graduate of Brooks Institute of Photography, has won many awards for portraiture and audio/visual presentations. His main areas of photography deal with commercial illustration, audio/visual, medical research, medical-surgical, portraiture, photojournalism, and public relations pieces. Recent exhibits include shows at the Los Angeles Art Museum, Hardy Gallery in Ephraim, and the Appleton Gallery of Arts. Ric has taught creative photography for six years at the University of Wisconsin-Fox Valley in Menasha. His free time is spent photographing in wilderness areas.

Dal Bayles
Milwaukee, Wisconsin
Milwaukee-based free-lance photojournalist specializing in news assignments for national news publications. On a recent assignment for *Time Magazine's* February 29th edition, Dal shot color photos of Lee A. Iacocca, president of Chrysler Corporation during the Chrysler plant closing. His work has also appeared in *USA Today*, *USA Week-End Magazine*, and *Newsweek*. Dal has been a stringer for United Press International for several years. He shot a winning photograph for UPI of a marathon runner being cooled off with a garden hose during a race. A former staff photographer at various newspapers throughout the United States including the *Kenosha News* in Wisconsin, Dal says his photography represents "people on location."

John S. Biro
Milwaukee, Wisconsin
As sales representative for MCP Company, Inc., John provides expert and capable assistance to those requiring quality color separations and printing. His training includes color scanning and electronic imaging on the Scitex Response System. As a self-employed photographer, John has photographed and produced numerous slide/tape programs including a 16 mm film documentary on the Guatemalan earthquake of February 4, 1976 for WTTW public television in Chicago. A graduate of Columbia College in Illinois, John's principal fields of competence are: advertising production, color separations, graphic design, instructor and photographer.

Charles A. Blackburn
Image Studios
Appleton, Wisconsin
As a photographer for Image Studios in Appleton, Wisconsin, Chuck's assignments consist of shooting for advertising, preparing annual reports and corporate brochures and department store fashions. He studied fine art photography for two years in Phoenix, Arizona before receiving his B.F.A. in commercial photography at the Art Center College of Design in Pasadena, California. His past experiences include publicity shots for Herbal Life in Los Angeles and shooting architectural images for Shin Pacific, Inc. in San Diego. Chuck was born in Yokosuka, Japan and says his interests are fishing, surfing, and martial arts.

Barbara Johnson Borders
Mount Horeb, Wisconsin
Full-time instructor at the Madison Area Technical College, teaching visual

Virginia E. Braley
Milwaukee, Wisconsin
A second semester photography student at Milwaukee Area Technical College, Virginia is an amateur photographer from the Marinette County area whose work includes capturing people on film. She owns property in the Town of Beecher in Northern Marinette County near Pembine.

Waushara County   **James Koepnick**

communications. Barbara says that, "Audio visual production is my specialty along with commercial art." Borders has been a free-lance photographer since 1978. Her published works include photos taken for a Wisconsin State Historical Society calendar, the *Wisconsin State Journal*, and for the U.W. Sports Information Services (football). She has also worked for several Madison-area multi-image producers such as 35 West and Wallibillig & Bestemann.

Mary Elizabeth Brockhoff
Marinette, Wisconsin
As photo editor for the *Menominee Herald-Leader*, Beth is responsible for producing all the local news, sports and feature photos as well as overseeing the darkroom processing of reporters' and correspondents' film. She has been published in the *Green Bay Press-Gazette*, the *Milwaukee Journal*, the *Chicago Tribune*, the *Cincinnati Post* and in many university publications. Beth is a graduate of the University of Cincinnati and also attended Xavier University. While at Xavier, she participated in a school-sponsored project that took students to Haiti where they worked in missions in the Third World country. "I kept a photo diary of the project from start to finish and the photos were published in the *Catholic Messenger*." Beth shoots with a Nikon F3 camera and uses many Nikkor lenses.

Mike Burns
Chippewa Falls, Wisconsin
Mike is an amateur photographer who has been interested in photography since he was in high school. He enjoys photographing nature and his interest in astronomy has led to astro photography, some of which has been published in *Astronomy* magazine. He often has opportunities to photograph weddings and he has his own darkroom. Mike is a sales representative for Lawson Products and he always takes his camera along. His other interests are sailing, skiing and music.

Todd S. Dacquisto
Ion Images Studio
Milwaukee, Wisconsin
Todd has been primarily involved in corporate, editorial, advertising and multi-image photography for Ion Images Studio. Editorial assignments he has been involved in consist of photo contributions to *Midwest Living*, *Wisconsin Trails* and *Milwaukee Magazine* as well as the *Milwaukee Journal*. His corporate accounts have been the Miller Brewing Company, Kimberly-Clark, Wisconsin Bell and Deere & Company. For over two years, Todd served as the principal photographer and associate producer for the 57 slide projector multi-image presentation entitled "The Spirit of Milwaukee" which has received national awards. Todd has traveled extensively to the Peoples Republic of China for the U.S. China Peoples Friendship Association

(USCPFA). He has produced an audio/visual presentation entitled "Passport to Friendship" for the USCPFA which premiered at the World Trade Center in September 1987.

Ilse Dietsche
Wisconsin Rapids, Wisconsin
Ilse, who was born in Germany, was given her first camera as a Christmas present when she was nine years old, and she has been recording life and landscapes ever since. She came to Wisconsin in 1967. She started photographing the state because "it reminded me so much of my homeland." Her published works appear on calendars and postcards and she has recently had a photo used for the cover of her county's telephone book. Ilse plays a unique trivia game using the slides she has taken in Wisconsin. She began playing this game with friends and now plays it for different clubs. Ilse has attended many photo seminars through the PSA and has won numerous photography awards for her images.

Gary G. Dineen
Milwaukee, Wisconsin
Presently a photographer at Marquette University producing photos for various public relations and instructional uses. Gary was a news photographer for three years at the Community Newspapers, Inc. in Wauwatosa, Wisconsin. Some of his more recent free-lance clients come from the Milwaukee area and are the Milwaukee Bucks NBA Basketball Team, Summerfest, and the March of Dimes. Gary's published work has appeared in such magazines as *Track & Field, News, Sport Magazine, NBA Guide,* and *Referee* magazine. He has also produced news, feature, and sports photos for twenty Milwaukee suburban weekly newspapers.

Chris Dorsch
Image Studios
Appleton, Wisconsin
Chris obtained a job at Image Studios in Appleton six months after his graduation in 1986 from the Rochester Institute of Technology in New York where he earned a degree in commercial photography. Chris' free-lance experiences mainly took place between the years of 1984 and 1987. His work at that time

consisted primarily of boat photography. Chris is originally from Green Bay, Wisconsin.

Patricia R. Fisher
New London, Wisconsin
Pat has her own photography business in New London called Lasting Impression Photography where she does portrait and wedding photography. She has also free-lanced as a Wisconsin wildlife photographer over the years. Pat's portraits have sold throughout the state of Wisconsin and have been published in national wildlife magazines. She does some photojournalism for the *New London Press Star Newspaper* and in past years has contributed pictures to the New London High School yearbook and calendar. From 1984 to 1986, Pat worked for Kiss Photo Laboratory in New London.

Douglas Green
Sheboygan Falls, Wisconsin
Doug's photo career began at the U. S. Navy Photo School in Pensacola, Florida in 1963 where he first shot stills. His next assignments were for the *Arlington Heights Herald* and for the *Mount Prospect News,* both located in Illinois. He also did some pictures for *The Paper* in Oshkosh. While traveling through the southern and eastern portions of the United States during his Navy career, Doug shot stills for three books: *Early American Homes, Gardens of America* and *Circus Book.* Today, he works as a free-lance photographer. He deals

Forest County   **Virginia Braley**

with corporate slide shows, feature stories, annual reports and house publications. He has participated in exhibits at Milwaukee Summerfest in 1970, Oshkosh Public Museum Lakefront Festival of Arts, and the Milwaukee Art Museum.

Suzi Hass
Ellison Bay, Wisconsin
"I have been interested in photography since the 5th grade when I used to follow my classmates around with a small, cheap automatic camera," says Suzi. But she feels that her real beginning was when she bought a used Minolta 101 from her brother-in-law. After that, people started to show an interest in her landscape images and she sold a few photos at a local gift shop. From that time on, she has been busy doing "all sorts of things." The past three seasons have been spent taking pictures for the *Door Reminder Vacation Guide.* Suzi's other free-lancing includes family pictures, weddings, senior class photos and anniversaries. This October, she will have a private photo show at the Meadows of Scandia Gallery in Sister Bay. She still uses a Minolta 101 and a Minolta 201. "I love older cameras," says Suzi.

Dennis Hemp
Hemp Photography Studio
Jefferson, Wisconsin
"I am basically a self-taught photographer whose interest in photography started at Johnson Creek High School when I was the yearbook photographer," says Dennis. Today, he owns and operates Hemp Photography Studio in Jefferson, Wisconsin. His studio specializes in weddings, pet and children portraiture, commercial custom framing and old photo restoration. Debbie, his wife, works with him. Dennis obtained some hands-on experience in darkroom work when he worked for the Como Photo Company in Watertown, Wisconsin. Dennis also finds time to free-lance for the *Watertown Daily Times.*

David Hermann
Milwaukee, Wisconsin
Upon earning an associate degree in applied science photography at the Milwaukee Area Technical College, Dave went on to become a free-lance photographer working mainly in advertising, editorial location photography and studio photography. He worked for Allen-Bradley in Milwaukee for four years as a corporate communications photographer. He shot travel location pictures, passport and executive

portraits, brochures, calendars and news releases in addition to performing various photo lab functions. Dave was a first-place winner in the 1987 and 1986 photo contest sponsored by WIPA. Two of his photos were chosen for exhibit in "Wisconsin Photography 87" at the Charles A. Wustum Museum of Fine Arts in Racine, Wisconsin. Dave manages to keep his photo knowledge current through practice and by attending occasional work shops or classes.

Ron F. Hoerth
Kiel, Wisconsin
A photojournalist for the *Herald-Times Reporter* in Manitowoc-Two Rivers, Ron has been doing photo pages, shooting special events and people in Manitowoc, Calumet and parts of Kewaunee counties for the past eight years. He was an honor graduate of the Layton School of Art & Photography in Milwaukee. Ron owned R. F. Hoerth Studios for 14 years. He did commercial public relations shots, indoor-outdoor recreation illustrations, aerial shots, and still life. His photography has been used in over 100

Marinette County   **Beth Brockhoff**

magazines, books and brochures. Elected to serve as the Chamber of Commerce president, Ron's other distinguished achievements include being a recipient of a Distinguished Service Award for the Miss Wisconsin Pageant and recipient of a merit award for his 30 years of active service as a Boy Scout Council leader. He is also an accredited judge for the Wisconsin Fairs Association.

William T. Hooyman
Reische Studio
Kiel, Wisconsin
Bill owns and operates Reische Studio in Kiel, Wisconsin. The studio specializes in studio and outdoor portraiture and has one of the largest

on-premises outdoor facilities in the state. Other photography includes wedding, commercial and restoration services. Bill was awarded the Fox Valley Professional Photographers Association's "Perfect Award" in 1984 and 1985. In 1985 and in February of 1988, he was honorably awarded by the Wisconsin Professional Photographers Association for exhibiting one of the ten best prints submitted for general exhibition in the state. He studied photography at the Winona School of Professional Photography and at Mid-America Institute of Professional Photography. During the past seven years, he has done photojournalism for the *Appleton Post-Crescent.* Bill currently holds a board position for the Fox Valley Professional Photographers Association.

Jennifer M. Huntley
Duluth, Minnesota
Currently, Jennifer is finishing her degree in mass communications at the College of St. Scholastica in Duluth, Minnesota, however, she spends any available spare time free-lancing. She has worked for WFRV-TV in Green Bay, Wisconsin, and for WDIO-TV in Duluth, Minnesota where she has shot and edited 3/4" video tapes of news, sports and weather stories for daily newscasts. In 1987, Jennifer took a second place award for a photo entitled "Loon Calling" for the *Minnesota UPI* . Jennifer uses a Nikon FM2 and three basic lenses. Whatever she uses, Jennifer has developed her talent well enough to have become known as an award winning still photographer. She has lived in the Duluth-Superior region for the past 30 years.

Peter Hybben
Menomonie, Wisconsin
Presently taking classes at University of Wisconsin-Stout Menomonie in advanced photography, Pete brushes up on his skills for his own studio which he has run for the past 10 years. "A large part of my business is portrait, wedding and commercial photography, although I do my fair share of free-lance editorial work for newspapers," he says. One of his newspaper assignments took him to British Columbia, Canada to shoot pictures depicting modern-day life on dairy farms. Pete has done just about everything in his photo career from album covers, shooting for catalogs, to producing billboards for a congressman. He attends numerous seminars around the country and has worked with some well established photographers throughout the years.

Jeffrey R. Isom
Oshkosh, Wisconsin
Working to complete his degree in journalism by May 1989, Jeff is also employed as a staff photographer at the Experimental Aircraft Association in Oshkosh. He has done photography for many clients including the Miss Wisconsin Pageant in Oshkosh, the Rocky Horror Picture Show in Milwaukee, and the Valley Queen II. He has been photo editor at the *Oshkosh Advance-Titan* and the *Marquette Journal*. Jeff's work has been published in over 20 magazines and newspapers. His images can be seen in two books: *Great Aircraft Collections of the World* and *Stunt Planes*. Jeff owns and uses more than $4,500 worth of Nikon cameras and equipment.

Thomas H. Jacobson
Viroqua, Wisconsin
After graduating from the University of Wisconsin-La Crosse with a degree in economics, Tom went on to graduate from Western Wisconsin Technical School to become a state certified law enforcement officer. Through his daily work, he was able to acquire numerous hours of photographic law enforcement and investigative training. The four areas of photography he deals in are: law enforcement, portrait, commercial and front screen principles. He now owns and operates a

general photography studio with two locations: Viroqua and La Crosse, Wisconsin plus the Wiscenes Gallery-Fine Art Prints in Viroqua. Tom teaches several courses in law enforcement photography for the Wisconsin Department of Justice at Western Wisconsin Technical Institute and teaches several courses to fire

Trempealeau County   **Robert Lieske**

services and law enforcement agencies on legal photography. His most prestigious assignment was to cover the Space Shuttle Launch-Mission 41. Tom, who was a recipient of the Wisconsin Traveling Loan Print Award, has received National Print Merits-PPA and numerous state and regional awards since 1972.

Donald R. Johanning
Madison, Wisconsin
Don began photography "professionally" in high school in Racine, using a Speed Graphic 4 X 5 camera, and his interest continued through college. His expertise was then used as a roving writer-photographer for the *Dubuque Telegraph-Herald* where he produced features for the Sunday paper for two years. Don made the transition from 4 X 5 to Rolleiflex to 35 millimeter Leica and Nikon during his 12 years with the *Daily Jefferson County Union* in Fort Atkinson. Through the years, his photos have won many awards in the Wisconsin Press Photography Association competitions and he has also served as an officer of the WPPA. In 1974, Don took a job as a public information officer with the Division of Emergency Government and moved to a position in the Tourism Department where today he does photo projects for the state. Don is currently working on a photographic nature book that is due to be released in 1990.

Gary C. Klein
Marshfield, Wisconsin
As a chief photographer at the *Marshfield News-Herald*, Gary's responsibilities include news photography, developing picture ideas, doing local picture page layouts and running the paper's darkroom. He also worked for the *Sounder* of Random Lake, the *West Bend News* and, the UW-Oshkosh *Advance-Titan* where he was photo editor for two semesters. The paper won the American Collegiate Press Pacemaker Award during his tenure. Gary was awarded an honorable mention in the 1985 WNPA photo contest and took a third place for general news and an honorable mention for sports action in the WNPA photo contest. Gary graduated from UW-Oshkosh in 1981 with a journalism degree. His work was chosen for publication in the book *Best of Photojournalism-8*, University of Missouri's Pictures-of-the-Year contest.

Curt Knoke
Image Studios
Appleton, Wisconsin
Curt, a graduate of Rochester Institute of Technology, New York, with a major in photography, started his photography career in Appleton. He was head photographer for the 1958 Appleton West yearbook, the *Clarion*. After college, Curt and his friend Ron Bricco purchased Walter Winski Photography located in the Zuelke Building and formed Image Studios Inc. The studio outgrew its office space and moved to new quarters on South Lynndale Street in Appleton where it is located today. After five expansions on this site, Image Studios has 18,000 square feet of space and has expanded its staff to 11 photographers and 22 support staff. Curt prides himself in having an excellent group of fellow employees and provides

them with a family-type atmosphere. In May 1988, he was awarded Small Business Person of the Year (service division) by the Fox Cities Chamber of Commerce and Industry in recognition of outstanding contributions to advertising and for furthering the industry's standards. When he's not at work, you can find Curt at Mission Lake in Shawano County working on his latest project--converting a barn into a home.

Gary G. Knowles
Madison, Wisconsin
Gary lives and works in Madison where he has served as the director of the bureau of communications for the Division of Tourism Development since 1979. Many of his recent photos have appeared in various Wisconsin travel guides including *Wisconsin Spring & Summer*, *Wisconsin Fall & Winter Escapes* and numerous other state publications. His work reflects the great variety of landscape, celebrations and architecture that make Wisconsin a favorite tourist destination. Prior to joining state service, Gary was a television and radio host/producer and free-lance photographer in the Madison area. In 1977, he developed an artistic technique for altering Polaroid SX-70 photo prints and he has exhibited his work extensively, winning many awards and honors. In 1979, he was the only U.S. artist included in the prestigious Royan Salon International de la Recherche Photographique, Cedex, France. Gary's work is included in numerous collections including the University of Wisconsin Memorial Union, the City of Madison Art Collection, the Madison Art Center, and other private collections.

Larry Knutson
Horizons Unlimited
Prairie du Chien,
Wisconsin
Organizer of the Crawford County camera club, Viewfinders, and owner of Horizons Unlimited, Knutson has also won many awards in photography since 1981. He was awarded first place two consecutive years at Octoberfest in La Crosse, Wisconsin. Later he went on to capture first place at the Wiekenberg Art Fest in Arizona. Larry won a first place and an honorable

mention in the Professional Pictorial Division, National Dairy Cattle Congress contest in Waterloo, Iowa and also received a special invitation to display his work at the Annual Wildlife in Art Third Show held in Des Moines, Iowa. He has done commercial photography for many companies, ad agencies, and magazines such as *Wisconsin Trials*. For two years, he has instructed classes in introductory photography techniques at the Southwest Technical Adult Education school in Gays Mills, Wisconsin.

James R. Koepnick
Oshkosh, Wisconsin
Currently, Jim is the chief photographer of the Experimental Aircraft Association, and he is responsible for a three-man staff and for supplying four international magazines with photography including *Sport Aviation*, the EAA's main publication. Free-lancing regularly for the *Milwaukee Journal* and doing work for the *Omro Herald* keeps Jim very busy. Before he joined the EAA, Jim worked at the *Oshkosh Northwestern* as a staff photographer. His published works include: *Life Magazine* (where his photo contribution led to his being named Man of the Year in 1981 by the Omro Area Historical Society), *Business Week*, *Chicago Tribune*, *Wisconsin Trails*, *New York Times*, *USA Today* and many more. The Wisconsin News Photographers Association awarded Jim a first place for a feature he did in 1980, and in 1981 he took a second-place for a photo essay. "I have also worked

Barron County **Judith A. Teske**

for the Wisconsin Flyers, Pepsi Cola/Lowenbrau Bike races, Sylvania TV, Oshkosh Tourism Bureau and the Oshkosh Chamber of Commerce," says Jim.

Wayne Konkle
Sharon, Wisconsin
Graduate of University of Wisconsin-Platteville with a major in industrial arts.

Wayne and his wife Barb do candid wedding photography and shoot for other free-lance accounts in Sharon, Wisconsin. Wayne's first artistic medium was woodworking, and his speciality was making wooden bowls. Several of his bowls were purchased for use and display in the American Embassy in Australia as an example of midwestern woodcraft. He taught high school arts and crafts for eight years and has been teaching woodworking since 1969. "I exhibit and sell photographs at major midwest art shows," says Wayne, "places like Ann Arbor's Street Fair, Michigan's The Old Capitol Art Fair, Madison's Art Fair on the Square, and Cardinal Stritch College's Mile of Art Faire in Milwaukee." He is presently working with several magazines and publishing companies that will publish several of his photos in the near future.

Bruce D. Krueger
Milwaukee, Wisconsin
Bruce's photography knowledge was enhanced by attending the Milwaukee Institute of Art and Design and the Milwaukee Center for Photography from 1979 to 1982. He earned a B.F.A. degree in photography and went on to win several awards including first place in the black and white division of the *Milwaukee Journal's* Kodak International Newspaper Snapshot Awards contest. Some of his pictures are in a collection of the Charles A. Wustum Museum of Fine Arts. In 1987, Bruce received the Arthur P. Haas Memorial Purchase Award from Wustum Museum of Fine Arts. Presently, he works at the Boston Store's advertising department processing and printing black and white roll and sheet film. He also assists photographers in product set-up, lighting, and set building, plus he acts as a fill-in photographer. Bruce free-lances for public relations companies when they need photography for brochures or annual reports.

Mark Kunstman
Image Studios
Appleton, Wisconsin
Mark graduated from the Milwaukee Area Technical College where he earned an associate degree in photography. He worked for 10 years at Ken-Mar House of Portraits and has

worked for eight years at Image Studios, both located in Appleton, Wisconsin. Receiving a special appreciation award from the WPPA was only one of the many positive things that has happened to Mark in his photography career. His work has been exhibited on traveling loans numerous times for the WPPA and Professional Photographers of America Inc. Since 1985, he has earned degrees from the WPPA beginning with an Associate Fellowship in 1985, then a Full Fellowship in 1986. This year, he will receive a master of photography from the PPA.

James R. Labre
Oshkosh, Wisconsin
Jim started in photography in 1957 as an apprentice with Zernicke Studio in Neenah. In 1961, he attended Winnona school of Photography for a course in commercial photography. The U.S. Army interrupted his studies when he served in a U.S. Army Security Agency with tours of duty in Turkey and Germany. In 1965, Jim returned to Winnona for courses in management and business. He returned to Zernicke Studios to pursue his first love, photography. In 1981, he joined the University of Wisconsin-Oshkosh's photographics team. Jim has received three Professional Photographers of America National Merit Photograph awards, he was in the WPPA's Court of Honor, and has twice been awarded the Fox Valley Professional Photographer of the Year. Jim's creative pictures have been published in a number of state and national newspapers and magazines.

Robert R. Lieske
Eau Claire, Wisconsin
Bob is an audio visual media specialist for the School of Nursing at the University of Wisconsin-Eau Claire. He claims he is an amateur photographer but his many photo awards portray a different picture. One of Bob's shots won a "Best of Show" in the KINSA snapshot photo contest sponsored by the *Eau Claire Leader Telegram* in 1987. That same photo went on to the national KINSA contest and placed a special merit award. Bob entered the KINSA contest for the same paper the previous year

and took a third-place award. Bob says he is looking forward to this ambitious book project because he is familiar with the area's "nooks and crannies." Bob works primarily in color prints and slides.

John Lewis
Apple Studio Ltd.
Appleton, Wisconsin
From 1964 to 1965, John was a Vietnam combat

Winnebago **Nicole Hoffmann** County

photographer in the U.S. Marine Corps and he was wounded in action. After Vietnam, John became a news photographer for KTVK-ABC in Phoenix, Arizona. While in Arizona, he earned a bachelor of science degree in mass communications at Arizona State University. But John didn't stop there. He earned a bachelor of arts degree at Brooks Institute of Photography where he graduated at the top of his class. For eight years, John was the administrator of photography at AAL in Appleton. In 1983, he started his own photography studio in Wrightstown, Wisconsin. Today, he is the owner of Apple Studio Ltd. in Appleton, Wisconsin. John has served as a board member for the Fox Valley Ad Club for two years. In 1988, the club awarded John 10 first-place Addy Awards and a judges' award for his work.

Brian S. Malloy
Wauwatosa, Wisconsin
Brian is a 1981 graduate of Brooks Institute of Photographic Art and Science. Since 1986, he has owned a commercial studio in Milwaukee that deals primarily with advertising photography. Before that, he worked as a commercial photographer for Batemor Productions. Brian has also put his photographic talents to other uses. For example, he did medical research photography for the Medical College of Wisconsin that provides photography for use by the Milwaukee County Medical Complex.

Charles "Chip" Manthey
Green Bay, Wisconsin
Chip, owner of Chip Manthey Photography Studios, deals in creative images for industry, advertising, audio-visual productions, narration, wedding photography and commercial aerial shots. He has a lengthy list of free-lance clients including assignments involving numerous well-known people such as Congressman Toby Roth, Vice President George Bush and the former Wisconsin Flyers Basketball Club. Another free-lance client is Heritage Hill State Park in Green Bay. He shoots stills for the park and produces slide shows for visitors. Chip's images are for sale at the park's General Store. He also worked for Mercy Medical Center, Oshkosh, in 1978 producing slide shows, taking still photos and training people in audio visual usage and production. One free-lance assignment of special interest to Chip was for the Bay Lakes Council Boy Scouts in Menasha. He found this a real treat since he had earned his Eagle Scout award as a teenager and he was familiar with scouting. Chip graduated

Walworth County **Wayne Konkle**

from the University of Wisconsin-Oshkosh in 1977 with a Speech, Radio, TV, Film teaching certificate.

Mary "Casey" Martin
Wisconsin Rapids,
Wisconsin
Casey is now marketing a variety of photo notecards and operates a free-lance photography business called Collage by Casey. She graduated from the University of Wisconsin-Madison with a B.A. in communications. Casey believes in becoming involved in community activities and she is the chairperson for the Wisconsin Rapids Area Chamber of Commerce Tourism Committee and was a contributing photographer for the area's

postcards. Casey participates in photo workshops whenever and wherever possible. "Travel, writing, and photography are my three greatest loves," says Casey. She is also employed at The Print Shop in Wisconsin Rapids in sales and design.

Thomas G. Marx
Apple Studio Ltd.
Appleton, Wisconsin
Tom Marx is an avid outdoors person whose interest in photography began when he took an introduction to photography course at the University of Wisconsin-Green Bay while pursuing a business major. Tom went on to receive his photography degree from the Milwaukee Area Technical College where his portfolio was judged second in the graduating class. After graduation, Tom was employed by a commercial photography studio in Green Bay, Wisconsin. He began as a photo assistant and worked his way to studio manager. After six years of employment, Tom accepted a photography position with Apple Studio Ltd. in Appleton. Tom created the photograph that took first place in the

1988 Addy Awards for Apple Studio. "I hope I can remain in Wisconsin because of all it has to offer to me from its beautiful lakes, rivers and streams to its vast amount of wildlife in its woods," says Tom. "Commercial photography isn't for everyone with the long hours and hard work, but I don't know any other way I could get to see and do so many interesting things. My assignments range from shooting the core of a nuclear power plant during refueling to the interiors of mansions in Cape Cod."

Carol L. Mason
Neenah, Wisconsin
Carol holds an M.A. in humanities with an art emphasis from the University of Wisconsin-Oshkosh. She has won many photo awards including a first place for Best Photo (voted by exhibitors) in 1986 at the Park Plaza Photo Show, a photo purchase prize from the Wisconsin Arts Board in Madison and an award from the Dodge County Correctional Institute. Carol served as the photographer for the Archaeology Department at UW-Oshkosh for three years. She photographed for the Oshkosh Earth Science Club's Annual Show for five years. She presently does a wide variety of free-lance work from graphic art drawings to photography. Carol is a member of the Appleton Gallery of Arts, Wisconsin Women in the Arts and the Oshkosh Fine Arts Association.

Carl E. May
Milwaukee, Wisconsin
Carl was a photographer and process camera operator for GE Medical Systems Operations in Waukesha for 14 years. His responsibilities included shooting half-tones, PMT live shots and clear film positives. In addition, he maintained and operated a Kreonite color processor and King concept film developer. Carl has done passport photography, visa and executive portraits, table-top still lifes, copy stand photography for flat artwork for Kodalith word slides and the production and development of multi-media slide presentations. His published work includes a photograph titled "My Glamourous Wife" that placed third in GE Employees' Photo contest and which appeared in GE's *Monogram Magazine*. Another was an article in the *Milwaukee Journal* featuring his exhibit "Little People." In 1984, he was invited to participate in Governor Anthony Earl's Black History Month exhibit. Carl is president of Freewheelers, an arts and crafts association in Milwaukee.

Dori J. McKearn
Janesville, Wisconsin
Dori's main area of interest has been in the exploration of color through paint, photography, and computer graphics. She works in black and white photography primarily but

Milwaukee County   John S. Biro

occasionally experiments with hand tinting. Dori had a one-person show of paintings, photographs, and computer graphic images in 1987 at the Janesville Country Club. She is a graduate of the University of Wisconsin-Madison with a degree in art.

Robert "Buck" Miller
Milwaukee, Wisconsin
Buck has been a staff photographer for the *Milwaukee Journal* since 1976. He has been nominated twice for the Pulitzer Prize. Some of his photo assignments appeared in such magazines as *Life, National Geographic, Newsweek, Time, Sports Illustrated,* and *Barron's Magazine*. In 1988, Buck received an award of excellence in the pictorial category judged by the National Press Photographers Association. He holds a B.S. degree in photography from the University of Southern Illinois.

Jay S. Moynihan
Ashland, Wisconsin
Jay is an attorney in Ashland, Wisconsin. His photographs have been displayed locally and are used in various tourism promotional materials for

Outagamie County   Carol L. Mason

the City of Ashland. Last summer, Jay spent one day shooting slides around Ashland for use as a rear slide projection background prop for a play which was being produced for the Ashland Centennial concerning the history of the area. "It was very similar to this book project's intent except it

took place in one city," says Jay. Jay's work is on display at the Windmill Gallery in Ashland.

Keith R. Myers
Ripon, Wisconsin
A free-lance amateur photographer who has had experience in aerial, group, wedding and reunion photography, Keith has a career that also boasts of active aviation pursuits. He taught photography for 12 years at the Fox Valley and Moraine Park Technical Colleges. Keith holds a master of science degree from the University of Wisconsin-Stout where his course work included many photography classes. He likes "people subjects" and likes to work in macro and micro photography.

Ron Page
Neenah, Wisconsin
Ron is the mid-day announcer at WIBA radio in Madison. He also writes full-length screenplays and television scripts ranging from dramas to sitcoms. For three years, he has been doing free-lance photography for the Experimental Aircraft Association Air Show in Oshkosh. His photos have been used by the EAA for various publications and calendars, and some of his

pictures can be found hanging in the EAA museum. Ron also free-lanced for the *Milwaukee Sentinel* and the *Milwaukee Journal*. He took a first place award in 1983 for a sports feature photo in the Wisconsin News Photographers Association contest.

Mark S. Picard
Milwaukee, Wisconsin
Mark is the only photographer at Ken Cook Company and he is responsible for producing photography for catalogs, sales brochures, owners' and technical manuals, and advertisements. In addition to his duties at Ken Cook Co., Mark owns a small photography business and produces original prints and posters which have sold in various galleries in the Milwaukee area. Mark has received many awards for his work including Best of Show from the Wisconsin Industrial Photographers Association in 1986.

Randal R. Potratz
Omro, Wisconsin
Randy has been an avid amateur photographer since high school where a photography unit in chemistry sparked his interest. After that, he took a few more photo courses at the Fox Valley Technical College which helped his talents blossom. Randy says that it has only been recently, since his enrollment in the New York Institute of Photography's professional photography program that he has seriously started to work on photography as a career. Randy's photos have appeared in the *Omro Herald* and the *Ripon Commonwealth* newspapers.

Louis H. Rivard
Menomonie, Wisconsin
Louis has been an active photographer for the past 18 years. The last six years have been spent working at the University of Wisconsin-Stout. For two years, he has been successfully making his photo skills available to many free-lance clients. Louis has refined his techniques through practice and is not afraid of passing the challenge to photograph people. "I am always at ease and prepared, because I know what results from what I previsualize," says Louis.

Ted Rozumalski
Milwaukee, Wisconsin
Named Newspaper Photographer of the Year in 1964 and 1965 for his photos of President John F. Kennedy's trip to Texas, Lee Harvey Oswald, poverty in the Rio Grande Valley, President Johnson's White House, Pope Paul VI's trip to the United Nations, and the Civil Rights Movement. Ted worked for the *Houston Chronicle's* White House

staff in Washington, D.C. when he took those photos on assignment. Today, Ted produces photographs for a number of Fortune 500 companies through his agent, Black Star Publishing. He also works as a corporate photography consultant providing photographic services to Miller Brewery's Corporate Affairs Department. EXXON hired Ted to photograph underground coal and uranium mines as deep as 600 feet. In March 1988, Ted opened the Milwaukee Gallery of Photography which is devoted to showing and preserving Wisconsin's photographic heritage.

Timothy B. Sandsmark
Eau Claire, Wisconsin
An active photographer for nine years, Tim is the photo coordinator in the Media Development Center at the University of Wisconsin-Eau Claire. He also worked for the Curecanti National Recreation Area (National Park Service) in Gunnison, Colorado, assisting with campfire talks, boat tours and he was the park's photographer. Tim's photos have been published in university publications, local newspapers, and local, regional, and state publications. He has judged many local photo contests and has, in addition, won his share of awards.

Gary Scheer
Waupun, Wisconsin
Gary and his wife specialize in wedding, family, senior and pet pictures. "We limit our weddings to 25 bookings per year plus the other work," says Gary. He worked as a staff photographer for the *Reporter* in Fond du Lac from 1976 to 1978. He covered news, sports and social events for the Saturday and Monday editions, and he developed and printed his own work. Last year at the Professional Photographers Association, Gary received many ribbon awards in the contests held at both the regional and state levels.

Sally Schulenburg
Milwaukee, Wisconsin
A newly-established free-lance photographer, Sally has been making images on assignment since fall of 1987. For four years, she was the yearbook advisor and photographer for Wauwatosa East High School. For three consecutive years, her yearbook photos won

awards. Sally is presently a head swimming coach for men and women at Carroll College, Waukesha, Wisconsin.

Carl Schuppel
Oshkosh, Wisconsin
Carl began his photography career with a Polaroid camera at *The Pewaukee Free Press,* the mimeographed newspaper he started when he was fourteen years old. The pictures were scanned on plastic stencils which allowed them to be reproduced without a half-tone screen. Carl photographed for the Post Newspapers and other local publications until he took an intensive six months to publish *Happy Birthday Pewaukee,* a 200-photograph essay of the people and events in his hometown during its centennial year. In Chili, Wisconsin, Carl was photo editor and process camera operator for the ill-fated weekly *Time Out Sporting News.* Presently, he's a staff photographer for the Experimental Aircraft Association, Oshkosh. Many of his photos are published in the EAA's various publications. During EAA's annual one-week convention, Carl is kept "up in the air" where he photographs other aircraft from his perch in a T-34 which travels more than 100 miles per hour. A number of Carl's photographs have won awards and have been published in other magazines.

Bob Shirtz
Oshkosh, Wisconsin
Bob has been a full-time professional portrait and commercial photographer since 1976 and he has his studio in his home. The Wisconsin Arts Board selected four of Bob's photographs for a permanent display at the Wisconsin Veterans Home, King, Wisconsin. He has won numerous awards at the local, state and national levels for WPPA and PPA contests. He is currently working toward his master of photography degree through the Professional Photographers of America and a fellowship degree through the WPPA.

James M. Slosiarek
Greenfield, Wisconsin
Jim is an aspiring free-lance photographer who has done photo assignments for the Justice Department and portfolio work for a Milwaukee actor and a local band. He received a second place in Fuji's color

print contest and two honorable mentions in the Cilento Student Photojournalism Contest. His goal is to work as a staff photographer for a major magazine or newspaper.

Stanley Solheim
Madison, Wisconsin
Stan is a photographer for the Wisconsin Division of Tourism Development and manager of the Wisconsin Film Office.

Ray Spicer
Oshkosh, Wisconsin
Assistant professor of art photography at the University of Wisconsin-Oshkosh since 1986. Ray was also a resident instructor at Tahoe Photographic Workshops in Truckee, California and taught fine black and white printing techniques. His 1988 exhibits include

Milwaukee County   **Dal Bayles**

Infinity Gallery, University Park, Illinois; Galex 22 Exhibition, Galesburg, Illinois; and Views and Visions, Golden, Colorado. As part of Ray's published accomplishments, he made promotional posters for the Tahoe Photographic Workshops which have been distributed internationally. Ray is a very particular black and white printer and strives for the best print possible.

Martin S. Springer
Menomonie, Wisconsin
Marty manages and coordinates the operations of the Photographic Service Unit at the University of Wisconsin-Stout. His pictures have appeared in local publications and newspapers as well as in the *Washington Post* and *News Week-On Campus.* As part of the Brooks Institute's Advanced Motion Picture course, Marty was required to work in a professional motion picture studio producing actual commercials, training films, educational films, medical films, and animated films. Marty graduated from Brooks in June 1973 with a concentration in still photography.

Michael K. Strook
Mayville, Wisconsin
Mike is a student at the University of Wisconsin-Oshkosh majoring in journalism. He has studied photography under Dr. Leroy "Skip" Zacher. Mike worked as a staff photographer for the UW-Oshkosh *Advance-Titan* for five semesters. He has been free-lancing for the *Oshkosh Northwestern,* the *Beaver Dam Daily Citizen,* the *Madison Capital Times,* and the *Mayville News* in addition to his studies and other part-time jobs.

Russell W. Stephens
Eau Claire, Wisconsin
A graduate of the University of Wisconsin-Eau Claire in art, Russ presently does video camera work, cable casting and some beginning directing for the Public Access Center Cable Channel 8 in Eau Claire, Wisconsin. His work appeared in the 1988 RSVP 13th edition *The Directory of Creative Talent* and in *NOTA* (None Of The Above) a creative arts magazine at the University of Eau Claire. Russ received the Silver Paletter Award in the 1982 *Milwaukee Journal* Calendar Art Competition.

Bruce Starszak
Starszak Associates
Kaukauna, Wisconsin
A confirmed Nikon addict and self-taught photojournalist who enjoys shooting in medium format with a 6 X 7 Mamiya as well as a 35mm Nikon. Bruce has a particular interest in architectural and people photography. He has won both first and third places in the black and white category (the same year) in the Kodak International Snapshot Contest and was awarded several honorable mentions in other categories before turning professional in 1984. For the past three years, he has hosted an Outdoor Photo Workshop at 1000 Islands Environmental Center sponsored by the Fox Valley Technical College. He enjoys sharing his knowledge with other photographers. Presently, he owns Starszak Associates and shoots a variety of assignments including weddings "because I enjoy it." Bruce says, "I like seeing people having a good time and I enjoy catching the moment and making them look their best."

Juneau County   **Stanley Solheim**

Stephen Sturtevant
Menasha, Wisconsin
A photography instructor for Fox Valley Technical College, Steve currently owns and operates his own photography business. SMS Photography was started in 1980 for the purpose of being a photo illustration supplier. Since then, the business has taken a local focus which includes weddings, portraits, advertising photography for area businesses and promotional slide programs for the local schools. Steve displays and sells his photography in two Neenah galleries: The Mitre Box and the Hang-Up Gallery. A current project is to chart and photograph loons for the Wisconsin Project Loon Watch.

Judith A. Teske
Holcombe, Wisconsin
Judith does her black and white processing in her own darkroom. She has had approximately 50 prints published in the *Week-Ender,* a local weekly newspaper. Judith attends photo workshops at the Peninsula Art School, The Clearing and Northland College. She is currently president of Photo Impressionists, a local photography club. She occasionally photographs weddings and anniversaries and presents slide shows to local organizations.

Richard W. Trummer
Madison, Wisconsin
Rick opened his photo business in 1985 after receiving his photography degree from the Madison Area Technical College. He is a member of the Professional Photographer's Association, the Wisconsin Professional Photographer's Association and the South Central Photographer's Association where he has won over 16 awards for his photography talents in the last year. In his spare time, he is an instructor at the University of Wisconsin Memorial

Union and teaches boudoir portraiture and portrait lighting. Rick's specialty is commercial and advertising photography.

David G. Wacker
Clintonville, Wisconsin
Dave is a second-generation photographer. His father started Wacker Photo in 1924. Dave moved to Grafton, Wisconsin, in 1962 where he taught science and photography and took over Wacker Photo. Later, he began writing and photographing for magazines and textbooks. Commercial illustrations led to his working with audio/visual production. A complete full-service studio was purchased in 1984 in Clintonville and was named Photography by J.D. Several of Dave's prints were selected for the National Professional Photographers exhibit in 1985, 1986, 1987 and 1988. A recipient of over 200 county, district and state photo awards, Dave's prints are hanging in exhibits in England, Germany, Hungary and Thailand.

J. D. Wacker
Clintonville, Wisconsin
J.D., age 19, is presently employed at his family's portrait/commercial/ wedding studio. J.D. does photography for University of Wisconsin-Green Bay promotional materials. He began his photographic career as a photographer for the *Ozaukee Press* in Port Washington, Wisconsin at the age of 14. Also at the age of 14, he sold his first national magazine cover and exhibited his work in Germany. In high school, J.D. received many photographic awards including top honors in the Wisconsin Associated Press High School Journalism Competition. He plans to open his own studio soon.

Chippewa County   **Peter Hybben**

Jim Weiland
Image Studios
Appleton, Wisconsin
Jim earned a bachelor of fine arts degree in photojournalism at Rochester Institute of Technology, Rochester, New York, in 1976. For two years, he worked as a staff photographer at the *Daily Pantagraph,* Bloomington, Illinois and the *Herald Leader,* Menominee, Michigan. Jim joined Image Studios in Appleton in 1978 and has been manager of the studio since 1982.

Philip N. Weston
Oshkosh, Wisconsin
Phil was a staff photographer in Germany for the 5th Corps Public Information Office which supplied photos to the *Stars & Stripes Newspaper,* other European publications, and the *United Press* and *Associated Press* wire services. In 1979, he became a part owner in Service Litho-Print, a commercial printing company in Oshkosh, Wisconsin. They provide high-quality multicolor sheetfed printing services including the printing of artists' reproductions, annual reports, and product catalogs. Phil was a 1971 photojournalism graduate of the University of Iowa.

Jeffery J. Wirth
Menasha, Wisconsin
Jeff is sole owner of Images of the Mind Photography and has had several of his photos published in local promotional brochures. He is a financial planner and stock broker for First Affiliated Securities in Appleton, Wisconsin. Jeff has also worked for several insurance companies and was part owner of Babbitt-Sholund Insurance Agency in Neenah. Jeff graduated from the University of Omaha, Nebraska, with a degree in business administration.

Richard Yehl
Milwaukee, Wisconsin
Dick is a full-time machinist at Evinrude Outboard, Milwaukee. He has pursued his interest in photography as an amateur since high school. Dick is presently vice president of the West Bend Camera Club.

Dr. Leroy "Skip" Zacher
Oshkosh, Wisconsin
Skip was born in Brookfield, Wisconsin, and he graduated from Brookfield Central High School. He earned a bachlor of science degree at the University of Wisconsin-Platteville and a master of science at the University of Wisconsin-Stout. Skip went on to earn a Ph.D. from East Texas State University. He has taught at the Frank Lloyd Wright Junior High School, West Allis, UW-Stout, and East Texas State University. In his 25 years of professional photography experience, Skip has produced, directed and coordinated numerous stills, 16mm, 8mm, television and multimedia programs. He has taught undergraduate and graduate photography classes at three universities. Presently, he teaches Press Photo I and Press Photo II in the Journalism Department at the University of Wisconsin-Oshkosh. In the past two years, Skip has published more than 250 of his photos many of which were taken while working for the *Green Bay Press Gazette* during a recent leave from teaching. His most recent activity, along with his teaching responsibilities, has been to serve as chief photo editor for *A Portrait of Everyday Life in Wisconsin.*

Contributing Photographers:

Nicole Hoffmann, 13, Oshkosh
Steve Platteter, Port Washington
Susan Rasske, Ripon
Heidi Rasor, Racine
Jane Tade, Oconto
James Taylor, Menasha
Gary Weber, Pewaukee

Fond du Lac County   **Carl Schuppe**

A Special Tribute
by Mary "Casey" Martin

Ilse Dietsche and her husband Dr. Wolfgang Dietsche lived in Wisconsin Rapids for the past twenty years. They hunted their land in Babcock and skied the slopes at Whitecap. Ilse and Doc traveled extensively throughout Wisconsin and their enthusiasm and love for their adopted home was apparent in Ilse's photographic essays which she shared with area clubs and organizations.

In January 1988, when the book project *A Portrait of Everyday Life in Wisconsin* was announced, Ilse was one of the first photographers to apply, and she indicated she would like to photograph either Wood or Iron County. While she anxiously waited for confirmation, Doc was also waiting for something special -- a new kidney. A long illness had finally resulted in the need for a transplant which was scheduled at the Mayo Clinic, Rochester, Minnesota.

While they both waited for good news, they shared the hope that a new kidney would allow Doc to once again live a normal life. They also shared ideas about photos Ilse might take. Doc had some specific ideas on a variety of possibilities. He even decided to let his beard grow again so Ilse could take his picture with his dog Benji. Finally, Doc received his good news and he went to Rochester for the transplant. The operation was successful and everything seemed to be on the upswing. Ilse received her good news, too. She'd been accepted for the project and was assigned Iron County. Everything was going right.

Then one day Ilse called me to say something was not right. Doc was rejecting the kidney and the doctors were concerned about infection. I drove to Rochester to visit Doc and Ilse, and we had a good visit. The nurse even commented that it was great to hear Doc laugh again.

We talked about the book and Doc was so proud that Ilse had been accepted, and he repeated his ideas for composition and subject matter. He even said he'd help Ilse write the captions. I, too, had applied for the project but had not yet received any word. Doc was certain, though, that I'd be accepted, and he was right. Shortly after our visit, I was assigned Jackson County.

When I called Ilse in Rochester to tell her my good news, she said Doc's kidney had to be removed. I drove to Rochester to visit Ilse, but I was unable to see Doc. The shoot date was approaching and Ilse was concerned about fulfilling her commitment to the project. We talked about the possibility of finding a replacement and she decided to ask Dick Yehl, a good friend of Doc's from Milwaukee.

Doc's condition worsened. The infection had spread and the doctors decided to remove his gall bladder. So, about three days before the shoot date, Ilse called Dick and he agreed to make the seven-hour drive to Iron County. Dick enlisted the help of another friend and co-worker who, after they got off the second shift at work, agreed to drive so Dick could sleep on the way to Iron County. Ilse still hoped to do some selected photos in Wood County, but she was torn between staying with Doc and fulfilling his wishes about the photos.

On May 6, Dick headed for Montreal, I went to Black River Falls, and Ilse came home to Wisconsin Rapids. We all had pleasant and new experiences. We met wonderful people and began new and, hopefully, lasting friendships. Ilse said it was hard to concentrate, but the change of scenery was good.

On Sunday night, May 8, Elsie Patterson called to inquire how Friday had gone for all of us and to ask how Doc was doing. His condition was deteriorating and he had not spoken for two weeks. Elsie appreciated Ilse's dedication to the project under such difficult circumstances and she asked if Ilse would object to a tribute appearing in the book, and would I write it?

And so here it is: a special tribute to Doc and Ilse for their enthusiasm for this project from beginning to end, and a tribute to friendships.

Dr. Wolfgang Dietsche, born May 21, 1925, died at 1 a.m., Tuesday, May 17, 1988. He will be missed by his family, his friends, and his patients.

                                    Ilse Dietsche

"If we see something all the time as part of our everyday experience, we can become numbed to it. In essence, we no longer see it. And yet, it is the most common and elementary encounters that reveal the very nature of our existence with powerful directness."

Richard A. Ballin

**Sunrise on the
Fox River**

**Outagamie County
Richard A. Ballin**

6:30 a.m. sunrise at
County Park.

Polk County
Greg Anderson

Above

"The bus is coming!"

Brown County
Curt Knoke

Right, top

Golda Meir Elementary
School, Milwaukee.

Milwaukee County
Ted Rozumalski

Right, bottom

Sister Mary Ivo and some
of her first grade students,
St. Paul Catholic School,
Wrightstown.

Brown County
Curt Knoke

21

Above

Wrightstown Postmaster Myrna Ebert raises the flag. She says she is the postmaster not the postmistress.

Brown County
Curt Knoke

Right

Aaron Sulman, a Lawrence University student from Madison, buys a Mother's Day card for his mom from Sandy Gadamus at Conkey's Bookstore, Appleton.

Outagamie County
Skip Zacher

Far right

Nancy White, Rhinelander, delivers more than 100 *Milwaukee Sentinels* and *Milwaukee Journals* each day.

Oneida County
Stephen Sturtevant

Springtime tree planting in Eau Claire.

Eau Claire County
Russ Stephens

Mark Sobczak, City of Milwaukee employee, spray paints white crosswalk lines at the intersection of North Water Street and West State Street.

Milwaukee County
Dal Bayles

Above and right

John Gesicki, owner of Gesicki Bar and General Store, Poniatowski. John is also the promoter of the 45 x 90 Club. There is a geological marker in Section 14 in the Town of Rietbrock which is the exact center of the northern half of the Western Hemisphere. It is here that the 90th meridian of longitude bisects the 45th parallel of the latitude, meaning it is exactly halfway between the North Pole and the Equator, and is a quarter of the way around the earth from Greenwich, England.

Marathon County
Charles Blackburn

Left

Photographer Chris Dorsch spent about seven hours fishing with Marvin Weborg, his son Jeff and cousin Paul Sanders. The Weborg family, Gills Rock, is a fourth-generation commercial fishing family. They fish exclusively for whitefish. The Weborgs fish six days a week for nine months of the year. Weather permitting, they also fish during the cold winter months. Chris says, "The Weborgs enjoy their work, and after spending most of the day with them, I found the water very compelling and attracting."

Door County
Chris Dorsch

Above

Gerald Marrazzo and Peter Pesch clean fish at the Port Washington harbor.

Ozaukee County
Dave Hermann

Left
Scott Hansen, an employee at Krueger Floral, Mosinee, holds an armful of roses. Krueger Floral is the largest wholesale warehouse of roses in Wisconsin. Roses inside the climate-controlled greenhouse are picked twice a day -- morning and afternoon.

Marathon County
Charles Blackburn

Above
Adams County
Keith Myers

Right

Wisconsin Capitol,
Madison.

Dane County
Gary Knowles

Lt. Governor Scott McCallum discusses some of the day's activities with Richard Masterson, his chief of staff.

Dane County
Gary Knowles

Judge William E. Chase at work in his office in the Ashland County Courthouse.

Ashland County
Jay Moynihan

2 East Mifflin Street, Madison.

Dane County
Gary Knowles

Above	*Right*
Northwest Mink Ranch, Bruce.	Three little pigs on the Harold Wahl farm, south of Menomonie.
Rusk County	Dunn County
Randal Potratz	**Martin Springer**

Roselyn Peters sits atop a 100-foot tower and watches for forest fires, an especially urgent task this spring since lack of rain has left northern counties exceedingly dry. Roselyn begins her day at 9:30 a.m. and ends at 8:30 p.m. Roselyn, who would rather be called a towerman than a towerperson, began her job on a part-time basis in 1974 and went full-time in 1983. To pass the time, she enjoys reading the Bible and playing her guitar. The tower is located on Highway 70 between Siren and Grantsburg.

Burnett County
Greg Anderson

Early morning hikers at Eagle's Nest at Big Bay Point, Madeline Island.

Ashland County
Jay Moynihan

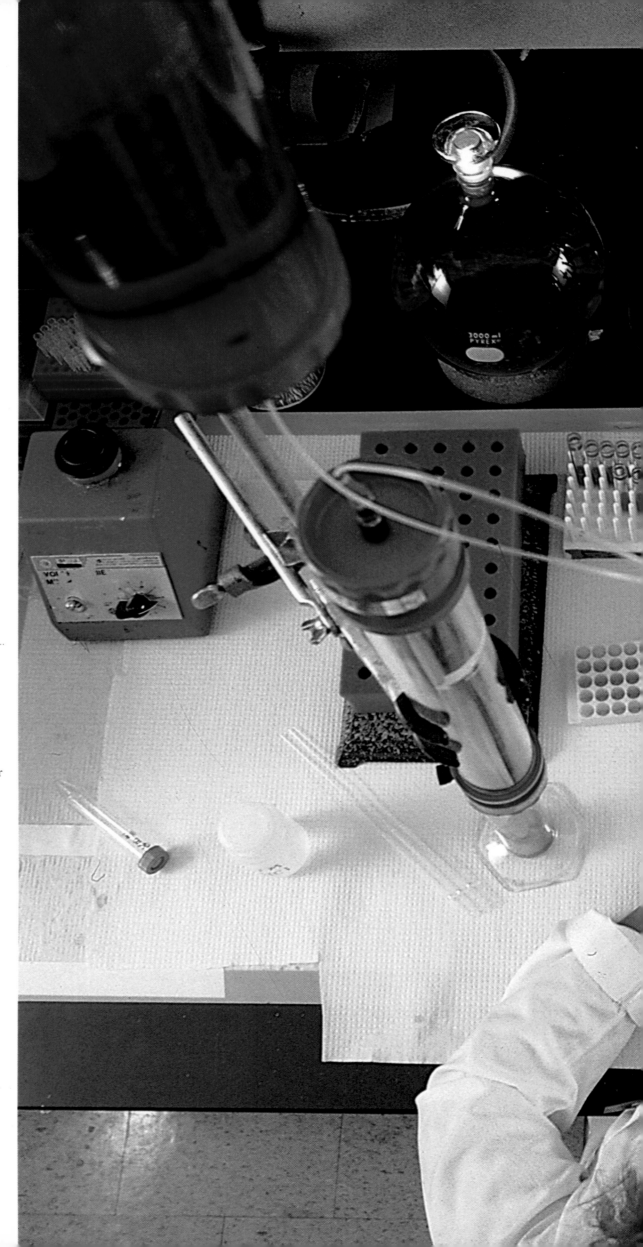

A lab technician at the University of Wisconsin Clinical Cancer Center, Department of Human Oncology works on breast cancer research. The lab, located in University Hospital, Madison, is renowned for advancements in research and education and is considered one of the most intensive clinical- and research-oriented cancer centers in the world.

Dane County
Todd Dacquisto

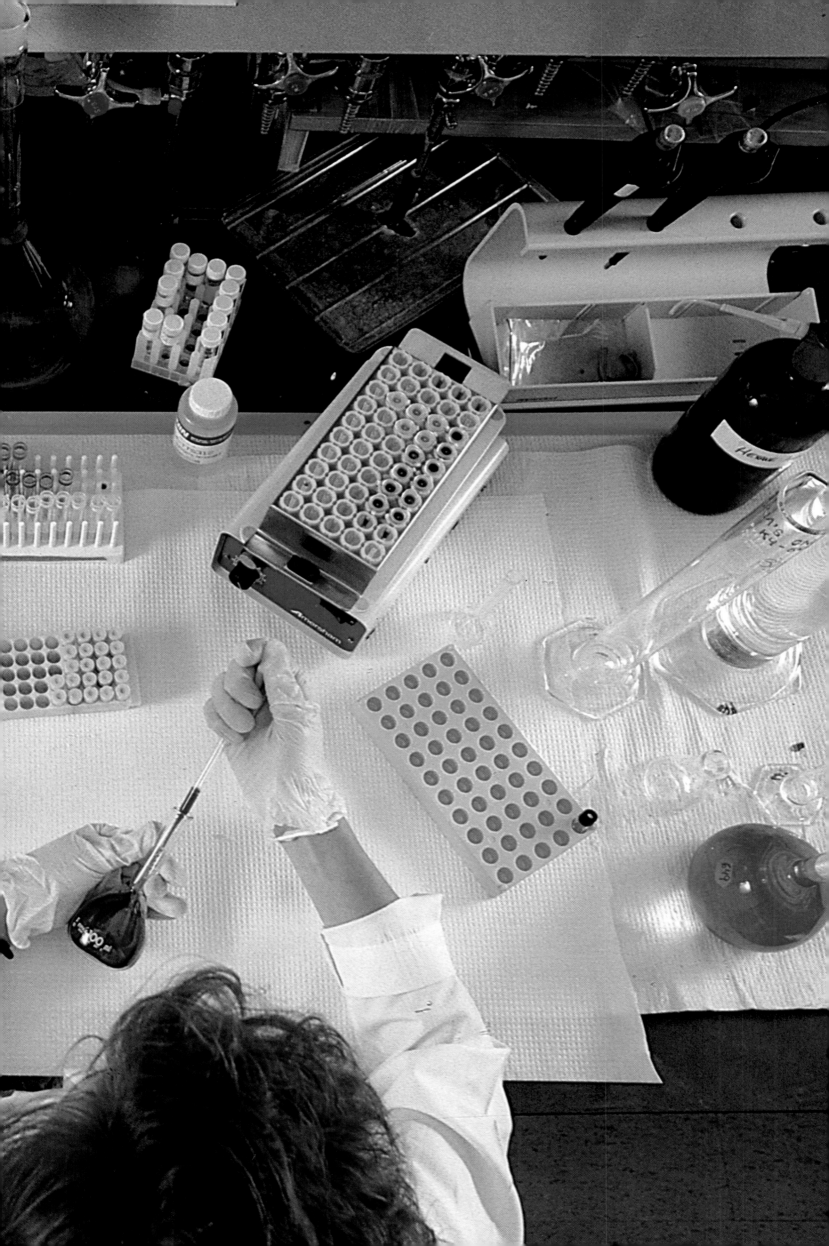

Above, top

On the eve of her big day, bride-to-be Merrilu Wheatley and her maid of honor Jeannine Williams check the final alterations of Merrilu's dress at the Wheatley home in West Bend.

Washington County
Gary Dineen

Above, bottom

At 4 p.m. on Friday, May 6, 1988, Julie Margaret Brennan married Mark David Koth at St. Gabriel Catholic Church, Neenah. Julie walks up the aisle with her father Douglas Brennan, Sr.

Winnebago County
Bonnie Auxier

Right

Brian Van Schyndel does a final check before the ceremony uniting him in marriage with Amy Meulemans at St. Paul Catholic Church, Wrightstown.

Brown County
Curt Knoke

Tour guides Dennis Hoffa and Audrey Wyman are dressed in historical outfits at Fort Folle Avoine. They portray typical fur trading situations for visitors to the site.

Burnett County
Greg Anderson

J. Hamerstrom, a wildlife biologist from Plainfield, with his friend Porfirio.

Waushara County
Ilse Dietsche

Far left

Al Auxier, 1984 Club
Champion at Ridgeway
Golf and Country Club,
Neenah, is reflected in
Prindle Lake as he
pitches to the number 5
green.

Winnebago County
Bonnie Auxier

Above

Senior citizens stay fit
and healthy by
participating in the water
aerobics class sponsored
by the Beaver Dam
YMCA.

Dodge County
Michael Strook

Left

Walworth County
Wayne Konkle

Right

Mary Rivard, Glenwood City, runs her antique shop from the oldest frame structure in St. Croix County. The building was moved from its original location in Crantown and retains the original name, Crantown Store. Crantown is now covered by water. The Rivards have an arrangement with St. Croix County to keep the store open to the public.

St. Croix County
Louis Rivard

book marks 50¢

Left

Bill Kratt, towmotor operator at the G. Heileman Brewery tapper storage yard, La Crosse.

La Crosse County
John Lewis

Above

Miller Brewing Company brew house, Milwaukee.

Milwaukee County
Ted Rozumalski

Right, top

Right, top

James Russell Aerts, Wrightstown, entered the world at 5:55 a.m. on May 6. Photographer Ric Ballin had made arrangements with parents Tami and Joe to photograph the birth, but babies wait for no one, and Ric was just boarding an airplane to do some aerial shots and he missed out on the delivery. He finally arrived at Appleton Medical Center to photograph Jimmy and his mom at 2 p.m. Jimmy was 21 inches long and weighed 10 pounds 12 ounces.

Outagamie County
Richard Ballin

Right, bottom

Eva Lorenz, who recently moved to Ripon from Iowa, is just finishing her laundry. She uses the time between loads to correct her high school students' papers.

Fond du Lac County
Carl Schuppel

Left

Paul Willems and Peter
Mrozinski, students from
a St. Paul, Minnesota,
grade school were part of
a group touring Crystal
Cave, Spring Valley. The
cave was bought two
years ago by Blaze and
Jean Cunningham who
are both trained
geologists.

Pierce County
Timothy Sandsmark

Kehl School of Dance spring recital at the Waunakee High School Auditorium. For 108 years, the Kehl family has taught dance to students from the greater-Madison area. The Kehl family originated in the city of Kehl, Germany, and descendants of the family have been teaching dance in Germany, Belgium and France since the seventeenth century.

Dane County
Todd Dacquisto

Area residents gathered at the Gifa Center, Gile, to plan a reunion of miners who had worked the iron ore mine. The mine, almost a mile deep, was the deepest underground mine in this hemisphere. It was closed twenty-six years ago and the miners scattered all over the country looking for work.

Iron County
Richard Yehl

Prairie du Chien Mayor Jim Bittner congratulates co-managers Mary Jane and Mike Faas at the the ribbon-cutting of the newly-opened 35-room Best Western Quiet House Motel. The motel is owned by Cathy and Bill Scholl, Elm Grove.

Crawford County
Larry Knutson

Right, top

White Bass Run on the Wolf River, Fremont.

Waupaca County
Skip Zacher

Right, bottom

The Kewaunee Nuclear Plant is operated by Wisconsin Public Service Corporation, Green Bay, and it is co-owned with Madison Gas and Electric and Wisconsin Power and Light, Madison. The pressurized water reactor, single unit plant is the largest of its kind in Wisconsin. The 535 megawatt plant opened in June 1974 and employs 225 people. It produces 25 percent of the power for northeastern Wisconsin.

Kewaunee County
Ron Hoerth

Far right

Steven and Cindy Kimball and their daughters Kerry and Ashley, Monroe, push off on the Pecatonica River.

Green County
Robert "Buck" Miller

Far left

Vic Saeger, machine tender, stands at the "wet end" of a Biron 26 paper machine, the newest and largest enamel printing paper machine at Consolidated Papers, Inc., Wisconsin Rapids.

Wood County
Ilse Dietsche

Left, top

Midtec Paper Corporation, Kimberly.

Outagamie County
Carol Mason

Left, bottom

Robert Przybyski, Neenah, operates a paper machine control panel at Wisconsin Tissue Mills, Menasha. Paper is produced at speeds of over a mile a minute with state-of-the-art high-tech innovations.

Winnebago County
James Taylor

A lesson in making blueberry muffins at the Whitefish Bay -- Shorewood Nursery School, Milwaukee. In 1948, a group of Whitefish Bay mothers decided that private schools in the area were not offering the kind of curriculum they wanted for their children. They wanted one run by the parents, where children as well as parents could learn. Parent contributions of special skills and resources could mean not only lower school costs but closer contact between home and school with a planned program under the direction of a professionally trained staff.

Milwaukee County
John Biro

Rick Meixelsperger is a baker at the Copper Penny Restaurant, Spring Green.

Iowa County
Brian Malloy

The main central control panel in the Miller Brewing Company brew house, Milwaukee.

Milwaukee County
Ted Rozumalski

Above

Painting the rotunda of the Grant County Court House, Lancaster.

Grant County
Larry Knutson

Right

The Green County Court House, Monroe.

Green County
Robert "Buck" Miller

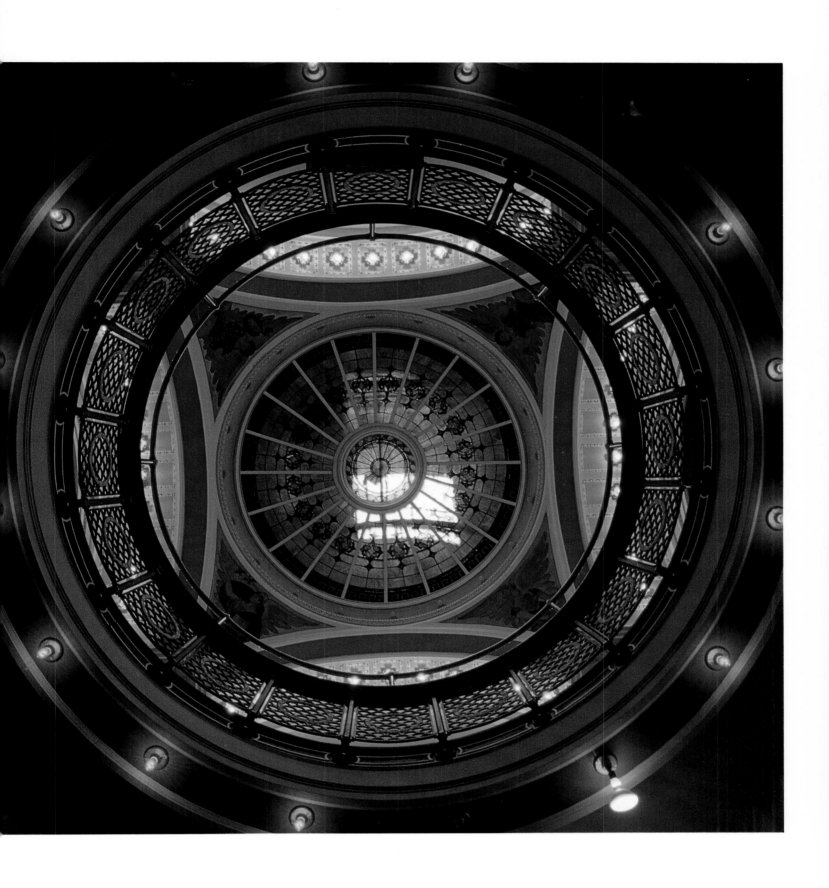

Above

Kenosha Fire
Department training
exercise.

Kenosha County
Mark Picard

Right, top

Burning off a field.

Waukesha County
Sally Schulenburg

Right, middle

Joe Pemberton, Town of
Iron River Chairman, sits
on the bumper of one of
Iron River's fire trucks at
the town garage. The
town has acquired seven

fire trucks, two
ambulances and two
rescue vans and serves
Delta, Oulu, Iron River
and Hughes townships.
Joe is a printer by trade.

Bayfield County
Don Albrecht

Right, bottom

Clinton firefighters had
two fires to battle on May
6. Here they have
controlled the fire at the
Badgerland Co-op,
Clinton.

Rock County
Donald Johanning

<table>
<tr><td>Left</td><td>Above</td></tr>
</table>

Left

Menominee Casino, Keshena, is Wisconsin's first and only gambling casino. Leslie Peters deals to Herman Gagnon.

Menominee County
J.D. Wacker

Above

Young entrepreneurs Elizabeth Bergstrom (center), Jessica and Emily Dery, Neenah, are open for business on a hot spring day.

Winnebago County
James Taylor

Right, top

Canoeing on the Kickapoo River near Ontario.

Vernon County
Thomas Jacobson

Right, bottom

Bayfield County
Don Albrecht

Far right

Crawford County
Larry Knutson

THE ONLY DIFFERENCE
BETWEEN TATTOOED
PEOPLE AND NON-TATTOOED
PEOPLE IS . . .

. . . TATTOOED PEOPLE
DON'T CARE IF YOU'RE
NOT TATTOOED.

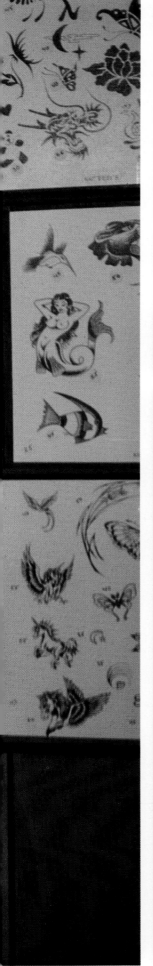

Scott Milde is surrounded by a few of the llamas raised on the family llama ranch in Sparta. "We have over 300 llamas here," says Scott. "Females sell for up to $10,000 and males start at $1,000. Their wool is much softer than sheep wool. Each animal can yield up to $400 worth of wool a year just from brushing."

La Crosse County
John Lewis

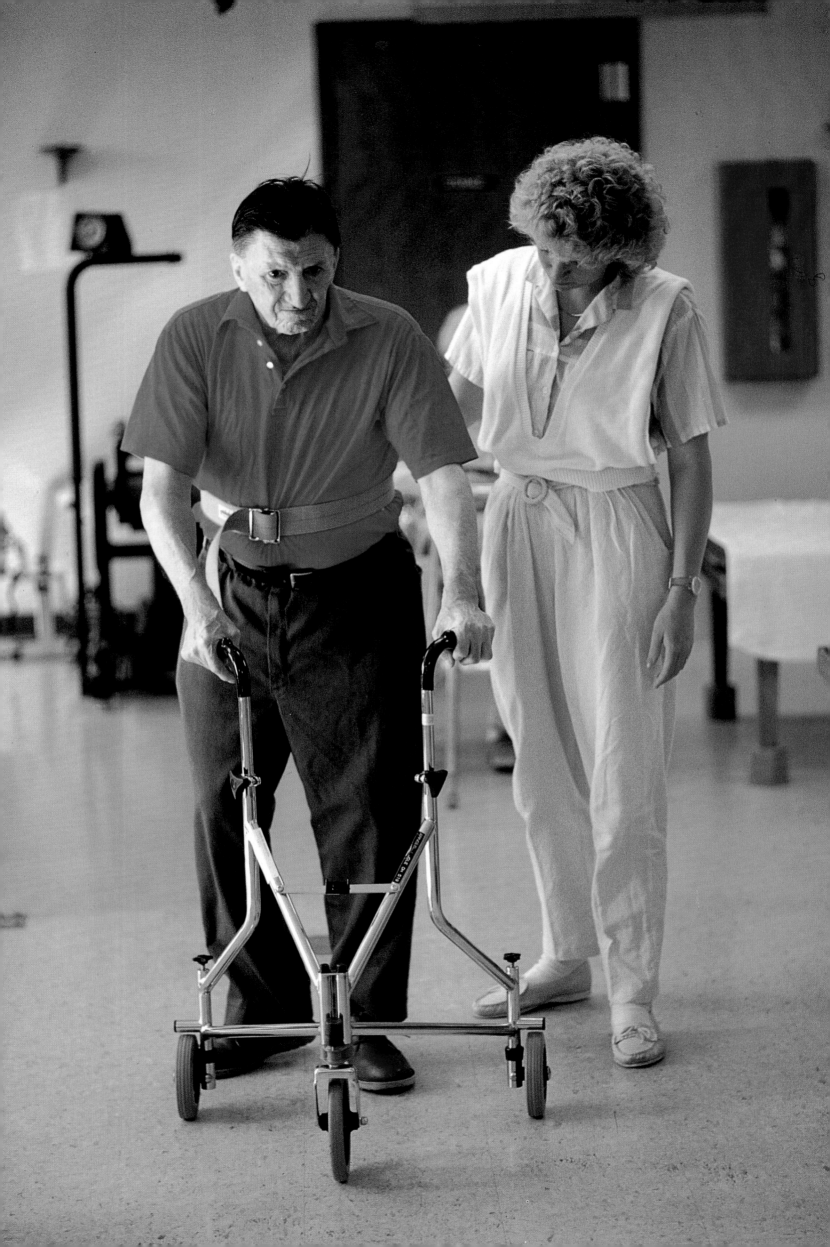

Far left

Jill Jenson, a contracted physical therapist with the Wisconsin Veterans Home, King, assists WW II veteran Louis Jellish with his on-going health maintenance program. Louis has been a resident of the home since 1983.

Waupaca County
Jim Weiland

Left, top

James Croatt prepares to raise the flag at the Ozaukee County Courthouse, Port Washington.

Ozaukee County
Dave Hermann

Left, bottom

City of Appleton Chief of Police David Gorski.

Outagamie County
Richard Ballin

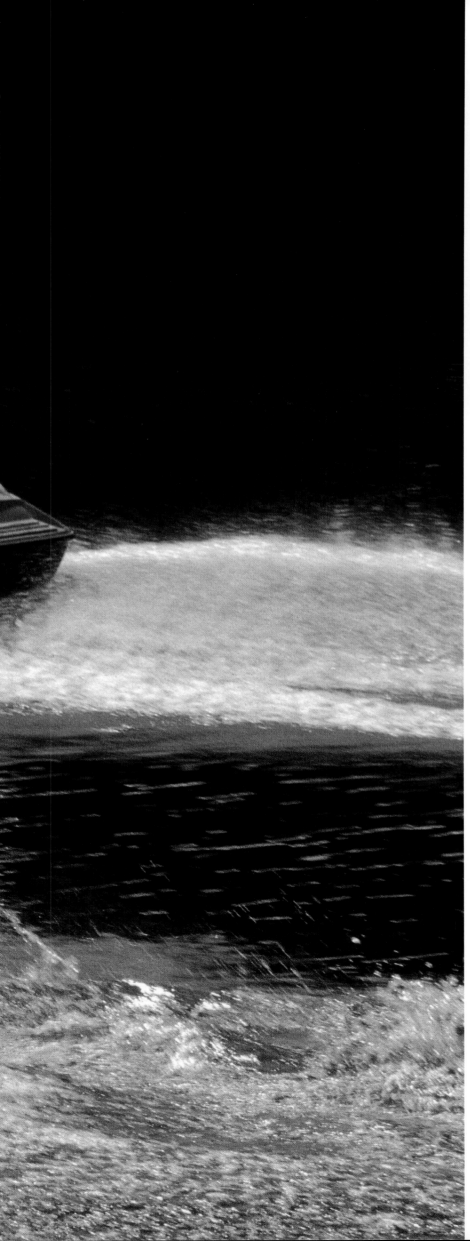

Left

Water skiing on the
Wisconsin River.

Columbia County
James Slosiarek

Above

Lake Geneva

Walworth County
Wayne Konkle

Left, top

For David Weinstein, 13, and Jerrold and Deborah Wicentowski, a Jewish Orthodox family, the Sabbath begins on Friday. The Sabbath candles are lit no later than 18 minutes before sundown. The Sabbath ends 42 minutes after sunset on Saturday.

Milwaukee County
Dal Bayles

Left, bottom

Fr. Michael Ciullo finds time for meditation in the Shrine of Our Lady Chapel at the Holy Hill Pilgrimage Center, Hubertus.

Washington County
Gary Dineen

Above

Amish women.

Vernon County
Larry Knutson

Above	*Right, top*	*Right, middle*	*Right, bottom*
George Colbert, Ashland, takes a break from operating his transportable car crusher.	Marvin Forton, draftsman for Terrace Homes, Adams.	Mary Lou Janish is busy making floral arrangements at Westfield Florist. Today, she anticipates working until at least midnight preparing for Mother's Day.	Helen Myhre, owner of Norske Nook, Osseo.
Ashland County	Adams County		Trempealeau County
Jay Moynihan	**Keith Myers**	Marquette County	**Robert Lieske**
		Barbara Borders	

Four curious students peek in the window while teacher Michelle Baryenbruch discusses a homework assignment with Joe Lobenstein at St. John's Catholic Grade School, Spring Green.

Iowa County
Brian Malloy

Far left

3M Corporation manufactures CD-ROM discs for hundreds of customers and applications at its Optical Recording Plant in Menomonie. These discs are similar in size and format to audio compact dics. Each disc can contain over 600 MBs of data which is equivalent to over 1000 double-sided 5 1/4" floppy discs. The disc is read by a laser beam focusing through a layer of plastic onto a spiral track of pits. These discs are part of a family of optical media products manufactured by 3M which include laser video discs, write once, and erasable media.

Dunn County
Martin Springer

Above

Westward, Ho! Children at the Porterfield Elementary School are dressed in western garb for the annual spring sing-along.

Marinette County
Beth Brockhoff

Left

Dolores Chandler, Chicago, conducts a gospel music workshop at St. Paul Church, Racine. "Gospel music is the root of the Negro culture," says Dolores. "The origin dates back to the days of slavery when the slaves sang as they worked the fields. It is the truest Black American art form still in existence today. All other forms of Black music are derived from this tradition."

Racine County
Carl May

Dori Kutt, Arcadia
Fryers Company,
Arcadia.

Buffalo County
Robert Lieske

Sportsman of Berlin,
Ltd., leather workers.
In the late 1840s,
Berlin was the hub for
fur traders and
trappers, and they
started a tradition that
continues today.
Presently, there are
twelve manufacturers
of fur and leather
garments in town
working in all types of
fur and leather.

Green Lake County
Bob Shirtz

Diane Harper wires a Cray II Computer. Cray Research, Chippewa Falls, designs and manufactures the most powerful supercomputer systems used for simulating physical phenomena. The computers are used for such scientific processes as weather modeling and structural analysis.

Chippewa County
Peter Hybben

The Tannery Lane Co., Rib Lake, fabricates skateboards out of pressed plywood. The boards are sent to a California manufacturer for finishing and wheels.

Taylor County
Jeffery Wirth

Above

Francis and State Streets, Madison

Dane County
Gary Knowles

Right

Lesley Blyth works on a stitchery project while listening to her friends Carrie Keller and Christopher Powers play the guitar and mandolin on the porch of their Pinckney Street apartment in Madison.

Dane County
Todd Dacquisto

Above

Dave Schaller works for John Diehl, Ferryville, as a commercial fisherman. This morning, he's catching catfish and other rough fish in the Mississippi River.

Crawford County
Larry Knutson

Right

Pecatonica River, Argyle.

Lafayette County
Robert "Buck" Miller

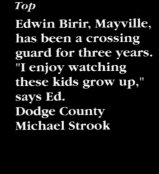

p

he first change of
ies at Harley-
avidson Motor
ompany, Inc.,
omahawk.

incoln County
atricia Fisher

Bottom

Construction workers
work on a new house
in Hudson.

St. Croix County
Louis Rivard

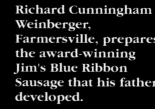

Top

Richard Cunningham
Weinberger,
Farmersville, prepares
the award-winning
Jim's Blue Ribbon
Sausage that his father
developed.

Dodge County
Michael Strook

Bottom

Jeff Martin, River Falls,
washes dishes at the
Truck Stop, Hudson.

St. Croix County
Louis Rivard

Above

Ann Kurz Chambers, Port Edwards, specializes in artwork that focuses on cranberries. She sells primarily to cranberry growers but finds that the general public is also interested in her work. Cranberry culture is a unique agricultural industry which adds $66 million each year to Wisconsin's economy.

Wood County
Ilse Dietsche

Right, top

Abler Glass, a decorative glass and restoration business owned by John and Bonnie Abler has been in business since 1976. Located in Kiel, their business has been called a "midwest phenomenon." Examples of their work include stained glass windows and Tiffany-style lamps. They have customers from as far away as the Chicago area.

Calumet County
William Hooyman

Right, bottom

Gary McCowen has been sculpting concrete lawn ornaments for 15 years. Gary says the average weight of one of his creations is 45 pounds, and prices range from $10 to $400. His work is available at Scott's Ornamental Concrete, Wausaukee.

Marinette County
Beth Brockhoff

Above, top

Tim Norris and Madeline Quigley, Madison, are welcomed to their campsite at Wyalusing State Park by park ranger Scott Sutton. Wyalusing, on the Mississippi River, is an ideal spot for birdwatching.

Grant County
Larry Knutson

Above, bottom

Inside the hull of a 38 foot boat under construction at Carver Boat Company, Pulaski.

Brown County
Skip Zacher

Right

Brian Tornberg, Tomahawk, paddles an inflatable raft on Townline Lake near Rhinelander.

Oneida County
Stephen Sturtevant

Wine bottled on May 6 at the Wollershiem Winery, Prairie du Sac, is packed in cases by Julie and Philippe Coquard. Wollershiem Winery vineyards were planted in the 1840s by Hungarian Count Agoston Haraszthy. The count left Wisconsin to begin winemaking in California and is considered the father of California winemaking. The count's vineyard manager, Peter Kehl, purchased the business. Peter's son Jacob continued the business until his death in 1899. In the winter of 1899, many of the vines were damaged by frost and the family decided not to replant. The Wollershiem family purchased the winery from Jacob Kehl's descendants in 1972. Wollershiem Winery specializes in oak-aged red wines.

Dane County
Gary Knowles

Left	Above, top	Above, bottom
Badger Paper Mill, Peshtigo	Oconto County	Oconto County
	James Labre	**James Labre**
Marinette County		
Beth Brockhoff		

Above

Lt. Chris R. Helstad and TSgt. Greg C. Ranum, Air National Guard, prepare an A-10 Thunderbolt II jet for an early morning mission. The A-10 has primarily an air-to-ground mission and its main weapon is a 30mm Gatling gun which is capable of firing 4200 rounds of ammunition per minute. Truax Field, Madison.

Dane County
Todd Dacquisto

Right

The Silver Rifles Precision Drill Team practices a drill for the Mother's Day Weekend at St. John's Military Academy, Delafield.

Waukesha County
Sally Schulenburg

Left

Green Bay skyline.

Brown County
Mark Kunstman

Above, top

Kelly Zwiers, De Pere, is having her portrait taken to surprise her father on Father's Day.

Brown County
Mark Kunstman

Above, bottom

At the Corner Store, Armstrong Creek, A.F. "Hap" Braley talks with Josephine Millan about the fun he and his wife are having while photographing in Forest and Florence Counties.

Forest County
Virginia Braley

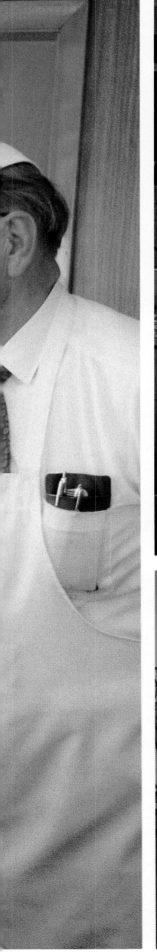

Far left

"What can we say about Rudy's in Brillion?" It's been called the "25 minute experience." Rudy Seljan has been serving good, homemade food for 49 years and he draws customers from many miles around. Rudy has never expanded his cafe but has always managed to feed a steady flow of customers and he goes that extra mile to accommodate them. Rudy says he's also beginning to think it's time to retire.

Calumet County
William Hooyman

Left, top

Kathy Anderson, a waitress at the Library Restaurant, Superior, serves one of the last meals of the evening. "After spending time with the staff at this busy restaurant, I'm aware now of just how hard these people work," says photographer Jennifer Huntley.

Douglas County
Jennifer Huntley

Left, bottom

Robert Skoraczewski, owner of Granny and Gramp's Bakery, Bayfield, prepares enough dough for two days' worth of donuts.

Bayfield County
Don Albrecht

Above

A fisherman launches a boat on Round Lake, 5:20 a.m.

Shawano County
David Wacker

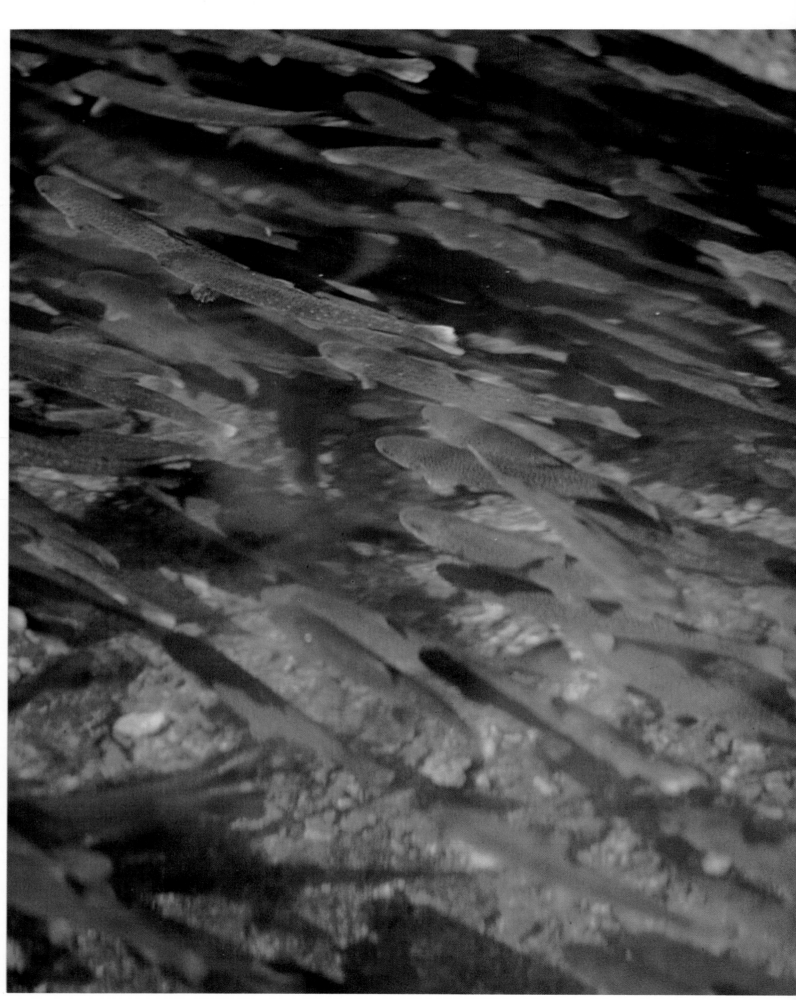

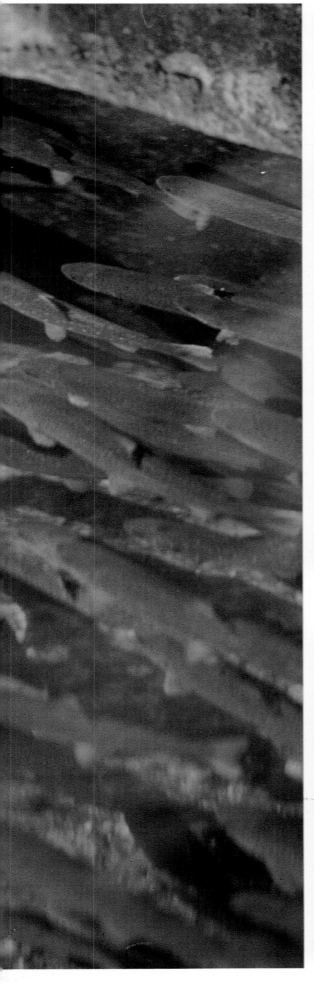

Left

The Joffrey II Dancers, Lissette Salgado and Adam Sklute, in "Grand Pas: Raymonda" performed at Lawrence University, Appleton.

Outagamie County
Richard Ballin

Above

Area children perform for family and friends at a spring dance recital at the Mayville High School.

Dodge County
Michael Strook

Above, top

Gathering eggs on the
Richard Koltz farm,
Greenleaf.

Brown County
Curt Knoke

Above, bottom

Dane County
Gary Knowles

Right

The Clarence and Gary
Boyke farm,
Fond du Lac.

Fond du Lac County
Carl Schuppel

Rita Sirota prepares smelt for the 16th annual St. Joseph Parish Smelt Feed. She says it's the biggest smelt fry in the area.

Sawyer County
Philip Weston

Roy Hoff prepares for a fish boil sponsored by the Branch Fire Department.

Manitowoc County
Ron Hoerth

Elizabeth "Coonie" Sarb, 89, prepares rhubarb which was freshly picked from her garden. She shared her favorite recipe with the photographer. Coonie was born and raised in this farm house and when she married Harry Sarb 64 years ago, he moved into her family's home.

Marquette County
Barbara Borders

128

Far left

Elizabeth Duacee Xiong, 3, Appleton.

Outagamie County
Richard Ballin

Left

Sheng Xiong, Sheboygan.

Sheboygan County
Doug Green

Below

Meephana Yanagg and family, Sheboygan, work together to prepare the soil in a community garden plot.

Sheboygan County
Doug Green

Right, top

It's a beautiful day for Sandy McCarthy to hang clothes outside to dry. Town of Manitowoc Rapids.

Manitowoc County
Ron Hoerth

Right, bottom

Karen Steigerwaldt finds shopping with her two youngsters quite a handful at the Ben Franklin Store, Tomahawk.

Lincoln County
Patricia Fisher

Far right

May 6 turned out to be a great day for Mary and Gearildean Cagle, Adams, to hold a rummage sale. They also have kittens to give away.

Adams County
Keith Myers

116

pants
50 and
up

shirts
25 and up

open

25¢

Left	Right, top	Right, bottom
Door County	Jim Heinen	Steve Knoop loads feed at the Shell Lake Co-op.
Suzi Hass	Sheboygan County	
	Doug Green	Washburn County
		Philip Weston

A Tomahawk High School student takes his turn at giving life-saving blood at the Tomahawk Armory.

Lincoln County
Patricia Fisher

Sgt. Rick Butz, Ripon, extends a greeting to a group of young people on Watson Street. Sgt. Butz has been with the Ripon Police Department for 10 years and makes an effort to walk his beat every night. He says it's important to know people by name and to interact with them.

Fond du Lac County
Carl Schuppel

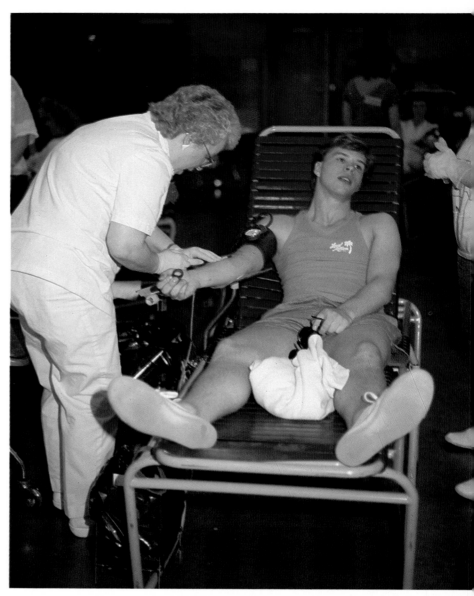

Below

Webster High School students decorate the Webster Community Center for their Junior Prom. Photographer Greg Anderson says, "It was kinda fun for me because they were playing the same Aerosmith tape we listened to ten years ago when we were putting up decorations for our high school prom."

Burnett County
Greg Anderson

Far left and left, top

Carnival at Winnebago County Fairgrounds, Oshkosh.

Winnebago County
Skip Zacher

Left, bottom

Glen M. Berg is a circus hand at the Circus World Museum, Baraboo.

Sauk County
Richard Trummer

When I finally found out
my father was right,
I had a son who told me
I WAS WRONG

Right

George Fabian, owner of the Park Street Shoe Repair, has been in the business for 28 years. He learned the trade from his father. George also repairs baseball gloves and hockey equipment.

Dane County
Gary Knowles

Left

Indianhead Sport
Parachuting Club,
Chippewa Falls.

Chippewa County
Peter Hybben

Above

Twice a day, Pamela
Murr, WTMJ Radio,
Milwaukee, boards a
single engine Cessna
plane and gives rush-
hour traffic reports to
commuters. In order to
get a real sense of
Pamela's work,
photographer John Biro
accompanies her on one
of her flights.

Milwaukee County
John Biro

Caddie Woodlawn Park, south of Menomonie, was the home of a young girl who lived during the Civil War. While all the young men were away, the women, children and older men were left to fend for themselves. During this time, rumors of Indian raids, which turned out to be unfounded, caused a great deal of apprehension

throughout the state. Caddie was eventually made famous by her granddaughter, Carol Ryrie Brink, who told her grandmother's stories in two books, *Caddie Woodlawn* and *Melon Magic. Caddie Woodlawn*, published in 1935, won the Newbery Award for children's literature and has become a classic. It was published in ten

languages and was reprinted 35 times. Presently, plans are underway to film a made-for-television movie of Caddie's life. Filming will start in autumn 1988 for airing on PBS Wonderworks. Tentative plans also include airing on the Disney Channel.

Dunn County
Martin Springer

Lillie Kolbe, 89, Glenbeulah, has lived in her family home since1901.

Sheboygan County
Doug Green

For many, the delightful song of the red-winged blackbird is the true sign of spring.

Clark County
Gary Klein

Above, top and bottom

"Untitled Landscape" 1986-87 was a project Joseph Beni says he personally felt needed to be done. The oil painting with metallic pigments consists of four panels 57" by 59" and took the freelance landscape artist a year to complete. Beni, who was born in Hungary, describes the work as a contemporary interpretation which plays with time, space, motion and light.

Sheboygan County
Doug Green

Right

A blazing fire was spotted south of Fond du Lac east of Highway 41 and less than a mile north of County Y. (Photo taken Saturday, May 7.)

Fond du Lac County
Carl Schuppel

Right, top

The Spirit of the Fox riverboat makes its way through the Menasha lock as it returns to its dock at the Menasha Marina. The Menasha lock is one of seventeen locks along 40 miles of the Fox River. This series of locks is one of the last in the world to be hand-operated. They make it possible to lower boats 167 feet from Lake Winnebago to Green Bay. From the bay, ships and boats can travel to waterways throughout the world. Today, this 100-year-old system provided the setting for a history lesson for the 150 students on board.

Winnebago County
James Taylor

Right, bottom

Jim Bauer and his children Max and Paula air-boating on the Chippewa River near Durand. This area is one of the few outside of the bayous of Louisiana and the Florida Everglades where air-boating takes place.

Pepin County
Timothy Sandsmark

Far right

U.S.S. Cobia, a World War II submarine, is a big attraction at the Manitowoc Maritime Museum.

Manitowoc County
Ron Hoerth

Above

"Turkey, anyone?" Steve Meier works for Northland Farms located in rural Chilton. Steve checks the coops twice daily for sick turkeys, breaks in the water lines, or any other problems that might arise.

Calumet County
William Hooyman

Right, top

North of Houlton on Highway 35 and 64.

St. Croix County
Louis Rivard

Right, bottom

S.C. Johnson and Son, Co., Racine. The building was designed in 1939 by Frank Lloyd Wright.

Racine County
Carl May

Far right

Marquette County Police officer Jack Frost radios for assistance because his brand new squad car is hissing and steaming. Closer inspection reveals it is only a problem with the air conditioner -- a relatively minor problem except that 82° weather is predicted for the weekend. Jack is a ten-year veteran of the force.

Marquette County
Barbara Borders

160

"Love you, Mom" - a
special remembrance for
Mother's Day, West Bend.

Washington County
Gary Dineen

Tobacco is left at a graveside outside of Keshena. It's an old Indian custom honoring the deceased.

Menominee County
J. D. Wacker

School children on the
Menominee Reservation.

Menominee County
J.D. Wacker

Above

Alpine Resort, Oneida Lake.

Oneida County
Stephen Sturtevant

Right

Robert Jones, Whitewater, enjoys a beer at a local bar.

Walworth County
Wayne Knokle

Left

La Crosse County
John Lewis

Above

Downtown Amherst.

Portage County
Jim Weiland

A field of flowers makes a beautiful foreground for Pete Alwin as he mows grass in North Freedom.

Sauk County
Richard Trummer

David Burr, Marshfield, is "having a heck of a time" attaching the wheels to the new lawn mower he is putting together for his parents.

Wood County
Gary Klein

Trucker Perry A. Gornjak polishes his cab in front of his Jackson home before hitting the road for Tank Transport, Inc. of Milwaukee. His constant companion on the road is a stuffed "Alf"

doll which was a Christmas gift from his sons Chad, Craig, Keith and Kyle.

Washington County
Gary Dineen

Right, top

Mostafa Ahmed, who is recovering from surgery, is comforted by his father Dr. Mahmoud M. Ahmed at Mercy Medical Center, Oshkosh. Dr. Ahmed was a resident at Mercy for one year but now practices elsewhere.

Winnebago County
Jeffrey Isom

Right, bottom

A patient arrives at Theda Clark Regional Medical Center, Neenah, under the care of EMS pilot George Miller and registered nurses Lori Lindeman and Joy Erb. Theda Star Aeromedical Network Helicopter is a part of the support and rescue team at the medical center and is one of three hospital-based emergency helicopters serving Wisconsin.

Winnebago County
James Taylor

Far right

Mary Manser undergoes knee surgery at Mercy Medical Center, Oshkosh.

Winnebago County
Jeffrey Isom

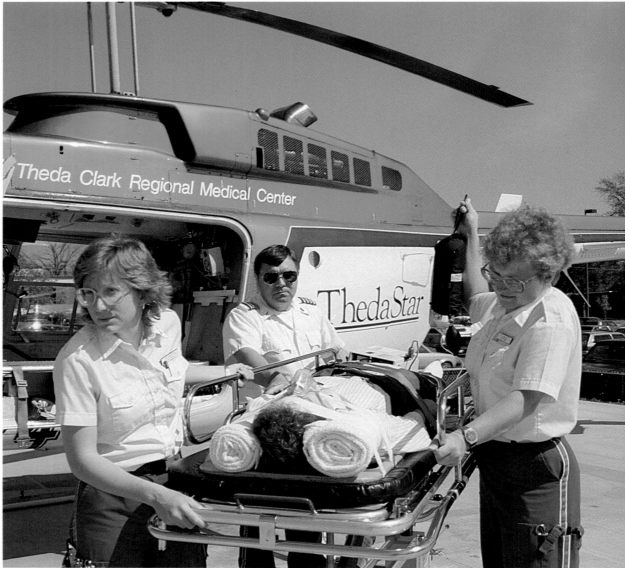

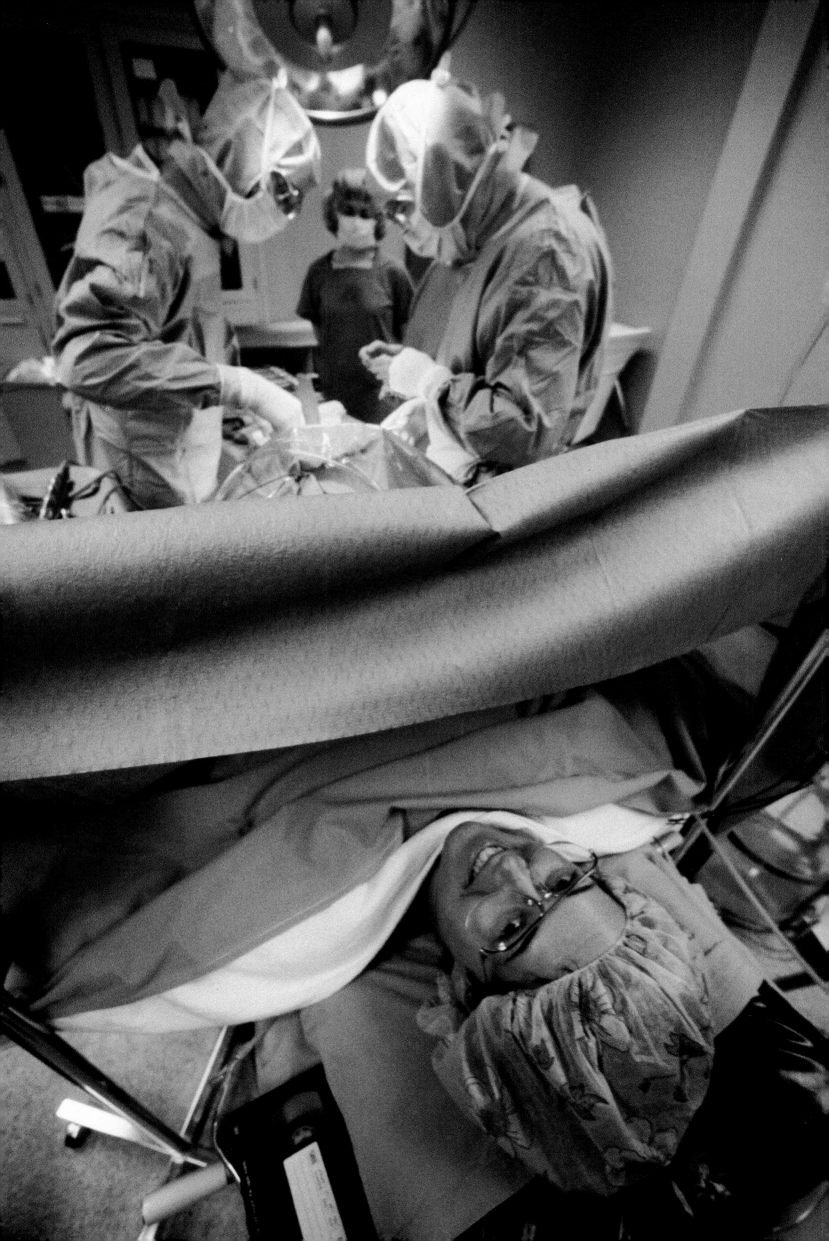

Right

Chad Feigley, 12, proudly shows off the rainbow trout he caught in the Little Sioux River.

Bayfield County
Don Albrecht

Far right, top

Fly-fisherman, Mark Glander, Richfield, Minnesota, tries his luck in the Little Sioux River.

Bayfield County
Don Albrecht

Far right, bottom

Sheboygan County
Doug Green

Left	*Left, inset*	*Above*
Dane County	Richard Koltz, Greenleaf	Cheryl Carrol gathers
Ron Page	Brown County	eggs on the MacFarlane
	Curt Knoke	Pheasant Farm,
		Janesville.
		Rock County
		Dori McKearn

Grain elevator at
Didion, Inc., Johnson
Creek.

Jefferson County
Bruce Krueger

Left

War for Sport is how
Edwin Paskey describes
his life-long fascination
with the military. Ed, a
West Bend resident,
realized his childhood
dream of serving his
country when he was a
member of the 34th
General Hospital unit of
the U. S. Army from 1942
to 1945. Since then, Ed
has continued to
surround himself with
military memorabilia
which marks his unique
brand of patriotism.

Washington County
Gary Dineen

Above

Edmund Seaman,
Adams, says, "The
money raised from
selling poppies is used to
assist needy veterans
who are hospitalized."
Ed served in both WWII
and Korea. For a
number of years, he was
a fireman in Illinois
before returning to his
home town. Due to old
war injuries, he has been
in a wheelchair for the
last seven years. He says
he gets around
everywhere in his van
which is fitted with a lift
and hand controls.

Adams County
Keith Myers

Left

A Lunda Construction Company welder works on bridge construction over Duck Creek in the Town of Howard.

Brown County
Mark Kunstman

Above, top

Sgt. Michael Jones, Sgt. First Class Bruce Weideman and Sgt. Al Ebert inspect tanks at Fort McCoy. The tanks are computerized and can detect body heat in a field several hundred meters away.

Monroe County
Gary Scheer

Above, bottom

Chuck Rodgers, Iola.

Waupaca County
Jim Weiland

This page and the next

Gregg and Sue Rasske, Majestic Balloons, Ltd., Ripon, offer the adventuresome a unique aerial experience over some of Wisconsin's beautiful countryside.

Fond du Lac County
Susan Rasske

Rob, Chris, Ted and
Sonny.

La Crosse County
John Lewis

Spectators at the Westby-
DeSoto Girls Junior
Varsity softball game.

Vernon County
Thomas Jacobson

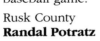

Above

Appleton East Patriots coach, William A. Diesch, cheers on his team in a double-header against Neenah High School. The Patriots won the first game, the Rockets won the second game.

Winnebago County
Bonnie Auxier

Right

Ladysmith-Flambeau baseball game.

Rusk County
Randal Potratz

Innkeeper Jerry Phillips sets the tables for breakfast at the Old Rittenhouse Inn, Bayfield. He had stayed up until 3 a.m. waiting for and greeting house guests from Chicago.

Bayfield County
Don Albrecht

James and Suzanne Kane, Burlington, have owned and operated Kane's Circle K as a side-line business for three years. They offer hayrides, sleigh rides and carriage rides. Along with their registered Belgian horses, they have a stagecoach and a covered wagon which can be used for parades, weddings and private parties. Suzanne is an ambulance driver for the State of Wisconsin and James is a die setter for Chrysler in Kenosha. When the plant closes at the end of the year, he will be out of work. He's looking forward to the continued growth and success of Kane's Circle K.

Racine County
Carl May

Left	*Right, top*	*Right, bottom*
Menominee Junior and Senior High School boys practice the drums in preparation for summer pow-wows. Menominee County **J.D. Wacker**	Spring Valley High School Band, Spring Valley under the direction of Jeff Roy. Band members prepare for the solo and ensemble contest to be held in Eau Claire on May 7. Pierce County **Timothy Sandsmark**	Tuba player Matt Lamb will graduate from Spring Valley High School this spring. Matt plans to attend the University of Wisconsin-River Falls in the fall. Pierce County **Timothy Sandsmark**

In exuberant celebration of the last day of classes, Jeff Rosenberg rides his bike off the pier in front of the Sigma Alpha Epsilon fraternity house in Madison.

Dane County
Todd Dacquisto

Above

Ed and Lucille Henschel, both 81, believe planting potatoes the old-fashioned way is still the best. The Henschels live in Antigo.

Langlade County
Charles "Chip" Manthey

Right

Central pivot irrigation system, Plainfield.

Waushara County
James Koepnick

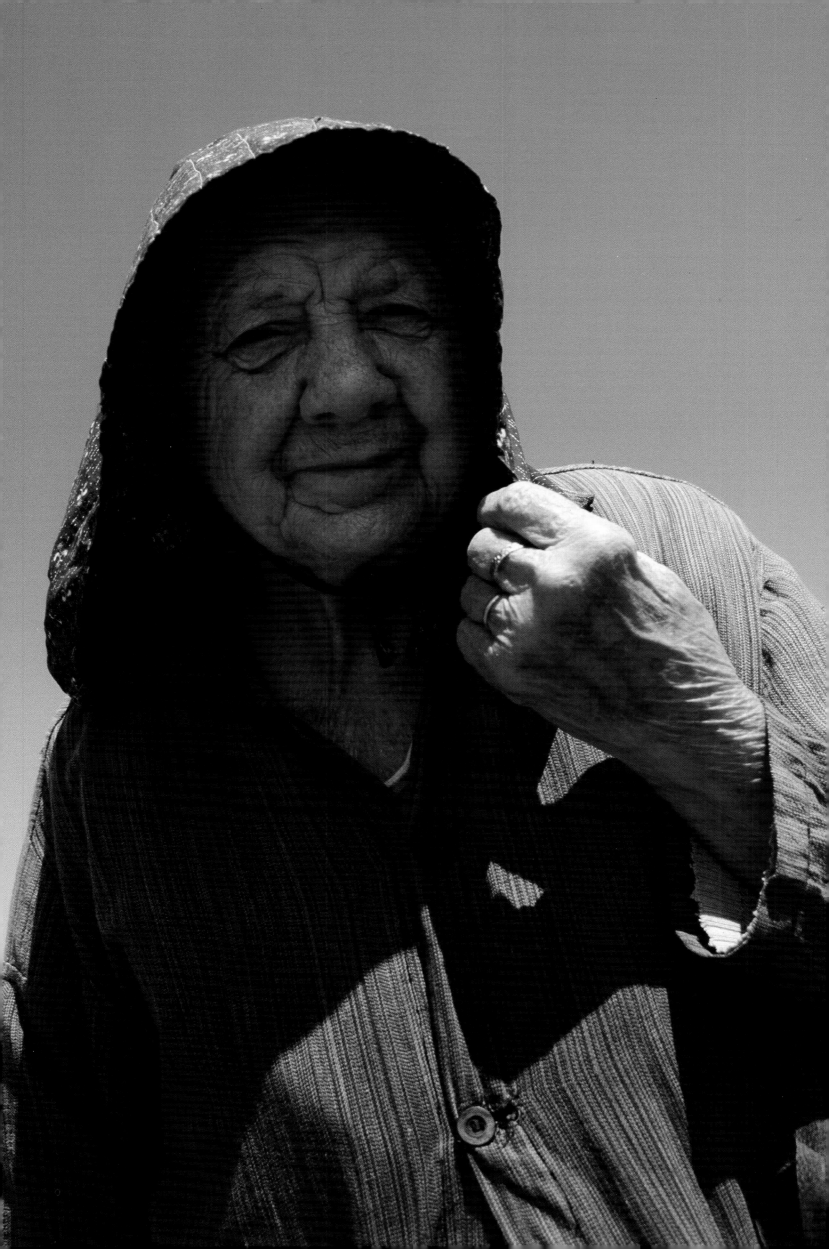

Cedric Dauphin is an exchange student from Cavillon, France. Cedric is a guest in the home of Rich and Pam Garmon, Neenah, and he's attending 5th grade at Coolidge Elementary School during a two-week student exchange program. The Garmons gave Cedric the USA hat which he wears all the time -- even during lunch in the school cafeteria.

Winnebago County
Bonnie Auxier

For Jackie Raehl, Neenah, it's hard sometimes to eat an ice cream cone without making a bit of a mess.

Winnebago County
Bonnie Auxier

Above

Cassie Stempel and her mother Nancy have come to Irvine Park for a picnic. Cassie has the day off from kindergarten.

Chippewa County
Peter Hybben

Above

Chippewa County
Peter Hybben

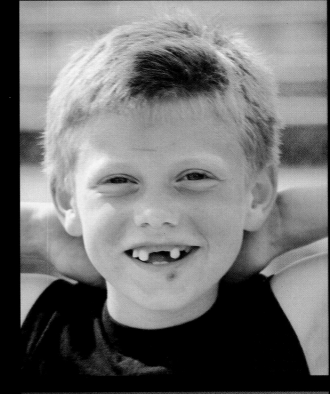

bove

arah Suprise, of
Korean heritage, is a
irst-grader at
Coolidge Elementary
chool, Neenah.

Above

Ian Klein, seven
months old.

Waupaca County
Jim Weiland

Lighthouse at
Kenosha harbor.

Kenosha County
Mark Picard

Inset

Russ Otterino works
on the light beacon on
Wisconsin Point. Russ
is part of the "Aids to
Navigation Team" with
the U. S. Coast Guard.

Douglas County
Jennifer Huntley

Right, top

Rasha, an Asian elephant at the Racine Zoological Gardens, gets a daily bath and foot care which consists of washing and an application of medicine to prevent the growth of fungus. The feet are trimmed once a week. Confined elephants can die from lack of proper foot care.

Racine County
Heidi Rasor

Right, bottom

Pilots Dick Rutan and Jeana Yeager at the dedication of the Voyager Exhibit at the Experimental Aircraft Association, Oshkosh. The Voyager was the first airplane to fly around the world without stopping or refueling.

Winnebago County
Jeffrey Isom

Far right

Stonecutters at Valders Stone and Marble Company cut stone which will be used for a breakwall to prevent erosion along Lake Michigan.

Manitowoc County
Ron Hoerth

Doc Eckes, Nelson,
paints a duck decoy.
Buffalo County
Mike Burns

Virgil McClelland,
woodcarver,
Menomonie. In 34 years
of marriage, Virgil's wife
Kate has never heard him
say, "I don't feel like
carving today." If Virgil
misses a day of carving,
he feels the day is
incomplete.

Dunn County
Martin Springer

Artist Charles Peterson, Ephraim, has lived in Door county for nearly 15 years. He has developed a national reputation for his watercolor scenes and wildlife paintings.

Door County
Chris Dorsch

Bob Eckels, the "grand old man" of the Bayfield Peninsula pottery scene demonstrates his skill at throwing a pot. Bob opened Eckel's Pot Shop, Bayfield, in the 1960s.

Bayfield County
Don Albrecht

Left, top	*Left, bottom*	*Below*
Diane Klatt styles Marcia Bloomfield's hair at the House of Fashion, Adams.	Wade Gundrum does bicep curls at the Vic Tanny Health Club, Waukesha.	Marilyn Hoffman and her daughter Ann, Black River Falls, give Lucky Old Hand a springtime shower and shampoo. (Photo taken May 7.)
Adams County **Keith Myers**	Waukesha County **Sally Schulenburg**	Jackson County **Mary "Casey" Martin**

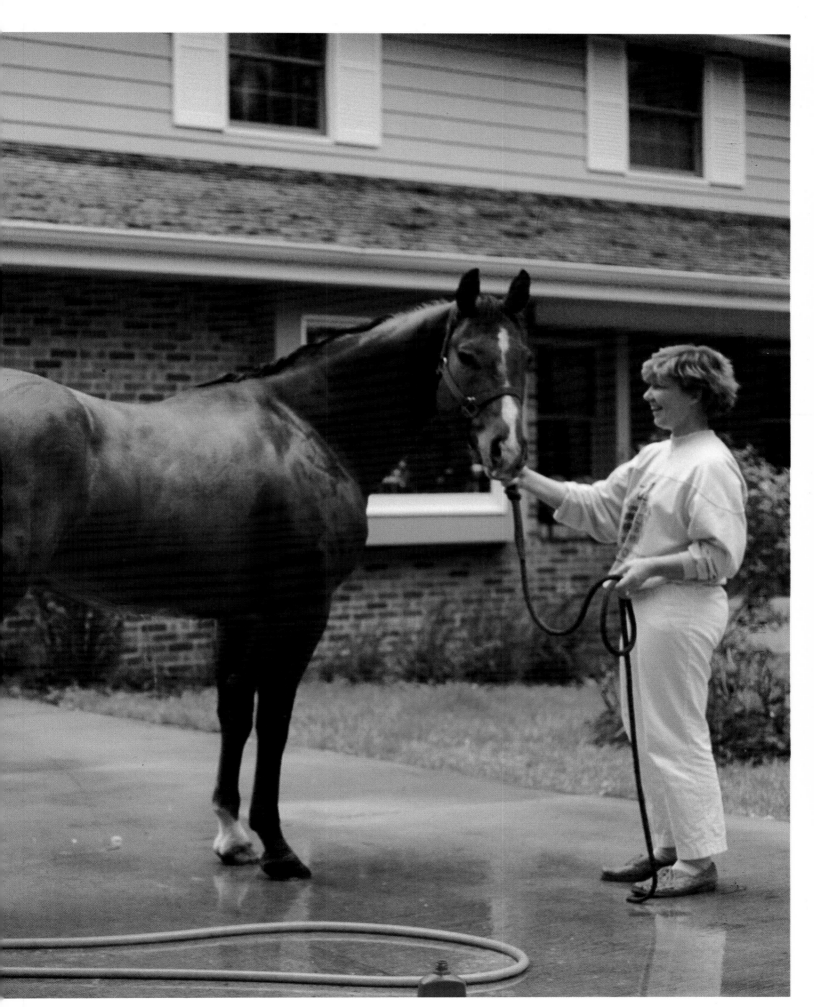

The Sew and Sew Club of the Tomah Memorial Hospital Auxiliary makes quilts which are sold in the hospital gift shop.

Monroe County
Gary Scheer

Allen Rogers, Robert Wicklund, Sam Welch and Eugene Rogers are four retirees who live next door to each other in Prentice. Every day they enjoy getting together to talk about hunting, fishing and politics.

Price County
Bruce Starszak

Right, top

Golda Meir Elementary
School, Milwaukee.

Milwaukee County
Ted Rozumalski

Right, bottom

When former physical
education teacher Wally
Mohrman moved from
Iowa to Bloomer, he
found rope-jumping in
the curriculum. He ran
into resistance from the
boys, so he started
having contests to see
who could make the
most jumps per minute.
What started as a class
contest has grown into a
regional competition
with more than 10,000
area students
participating. Bloomer is
the self-proclaimed rope-
jumping capitol of the
world, and competitors
have been featured on
the *Tonight Show, Real
People, The Harry
Reasoner Show,* and *On
the Road with Charles
Kuralt.*

Chippewa County
Peter Hybben

Far right

Valders Elementary
School children during
recess.

Manitowoc County
Ron Hoerth

218

After dark in
downtown Sturgeon
Bay

Door County
Suzi Hass

Below, top

Vernon Young uses his horses every day on his farm near Barron.

Barron County
Judith Teske

Below, bottom

Amherst

Portage County
Ray Spicer

Below, right

Eugene Bahr, Route # 1, La Crosse. Eugene and his family have been farming for four generations. He says of the upcoming fall elections, "There isn't much of a choice for the farmer. There are still tough times ahead."

La Crosse County
John Lewis

Above, top

Locomotive at the Railroad Museum, North Freedom.

Sauk County
Richard Trummer

Above, bottom

Clamming hooks used on the Mississippi River. When a hook comes in contact with a clam, the clam's muscles contract and grab onto the hooks.

Crawford County
Larry Knutson

Right

Lake Geneva

Walworth County
Wayne Konkle

Left	Above, top	Above, bottom

Alfred Gorr repairs shoes at his shop in Frederic. Initially, Mr. Gorr also repaired watches, but the move to digital watches and computer chips forced him to specialize in repairing shoes instead.

Polk County
Greg Anderson

Photographer Bonnie Auxier was listening to the radio while driving between assignments. WNAM announcer Bob Collins, Neenah, was commenting that since more than 70 photographers were out and around that day, surely one of them should stop in and take his picture. So, Bonnie drove to the station and did just that. While she was there, Bob talked her into doing an on-air interview to tell the audience about her day and what she was photographing.

Winnebago County
Bonnie Auxier

Volunteers tend the phones at the Channel 10/36, Milwaukee, fund raiser. Donated items are auctioned off to the highest bidder.

Milwaukee County
John Biro

At Badger Alloys, Milwaukee, molten stainless steel is poured into a cast. Badger Alloys is a sand and centrifugal foundry which primarily makes castings for fluid-handling pumps.

Milwaukee County
Dal Bayles

234

Far left

John O. Norquist was elected the 37th mayor of Milwaukee in April 1988 after thirteen years in the Wisconsin legislature. Mayor Norquist, 38, is a University of Wisconsin-Madison graduate and served for six years in the Army Reserves. "Every day I've been mayor has been challenging. This city is a wonderful place to live, to work and to raise children. The festivals, ethnic diversity and variety of art and music make Milwaukee a truly great place to live or visit."

Milwaukee County
Ted Rozumalski

Above

Menominee Indian Tribal Chairman Apesanahkwat at his office in Keshena. He is very enthusiastic about promoting tribal affairs and telling about the Menominee heritage, traditions and present-day problems. He also enjoys discussing everyday life on the "res".

Menominee County
J.D. Wacker

Left

City of Appleton Mayor Dorothy Johnson was elected to her third four-year term on April 5. "Appleton, the hub of the Fox River Valley, represents what is best about living in middle America. No wonder this is the fastest growing community in the state!" says Mayor Johnson.

Outagamie County
Richard Ballin

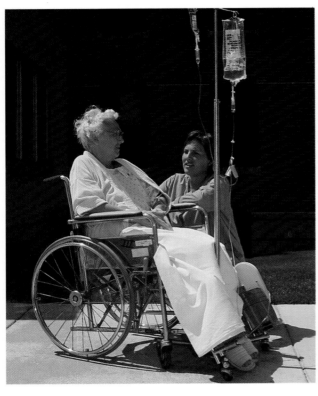

Above

Three days after surgery, Violet Dietz enjoys a moment outdoors with Barb Charlton at St. Mary's Hospital in Port Washington. Nurse Charlton notes that May 6 is National Nurse's Day.

Ozaukee County
Steve Platteter

Right

Donald Goldbeck fishes alone on the Black River. "I had surgery recently and I've been out of work for awhile. I like the solitude of fishing, but nothing's biting today."

La Crosse County
John Lewis

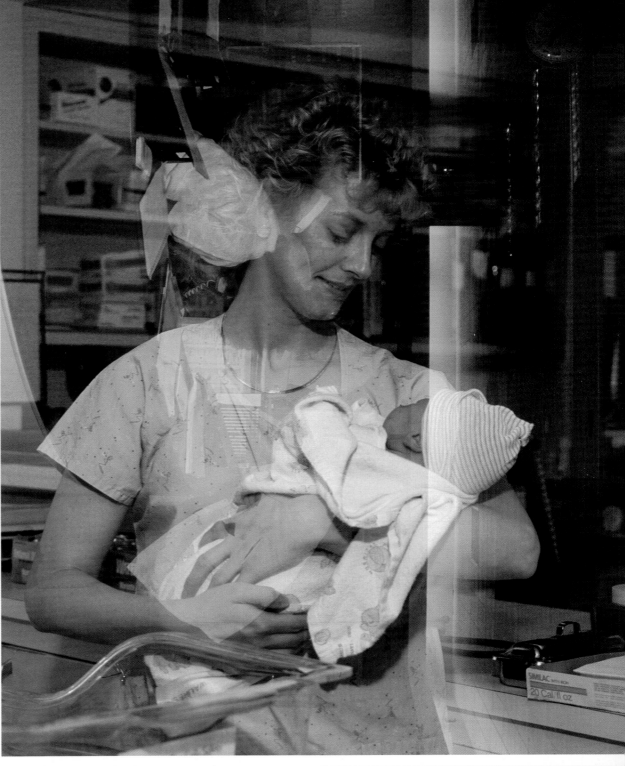

Above, left

Nelle Kopacz sits at the loom in the Old Court House Museum, Hurley, where she says she and her friend Lillian Kostac have woven 6000 rag rugs in the last six years. The rugs are sold to raise funds for the museum.

Iron County
Richard Yehl

Far left

Elaine Reetz, 68, is a freelance writer from Neshkoro. She also writes historical books on Wisconsin and on farming in Waushara County. Elaine has 36 scrap books containing everything she has written in the last 23 years. "There isn't a day goes by that I don't write about something," she says.

Waushara County
James Koepnick

Left

Woodcarver Jerry Holter moved to Clam Lake from Crystal Lake, Illinois in 1969. Though he calls himself a "wood butcher", Jerry has the distinction of being the only woodcarver in U. S. recorded history to carve a complete statue out of one piece of wood or tree trunk. Jerry, who is of Norwegian descent, has carved violins and cigar store Indians - that is, until public distaste, in the form of burning them, forced him into other types of carving. Jerry began carving fifty-one years ago when he was seven years old.

Ashland County
Philip Weston

Above

Old lumber mill, Tillida.

Shawano County
David Wacker

243

247

Right, top

Westby-DeSoto Girls
Junior Varsity softball
game.

Vernon County
Thomas Jacobson

Right, middle

Ladysmith-Flambeau
baseball game.

Rusk County
Randal Potratz

Right, bottom

Little League practice,
Polar.

Langlade County
**Charles "Chip"
Manthey**

Far right

Rev. Steve Scrabeck
coaches the Cornell Little
League Braves at Cornell
Mill Yard Park. "What a
wonderful, patient
coach!" says
photographer Pete
Hybben.

Chippewa County
Peter Hybben

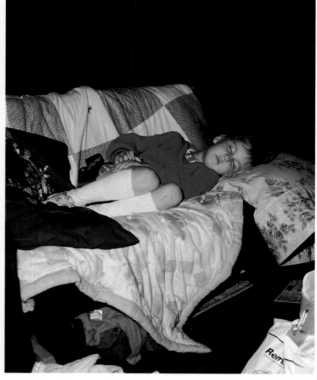

Northern Lights, 1:30
a.m., Neshkoro.

Waushara County
James Koepnick

Lake Winnebago
Winnebago County
Jeffrey Isom